Chasing the American Dream in China

Asian American Studies Today
Series Editor: Huping Ling, Truman State University

The Asian American Studies Today series publishes quality books on cutting-edge themes and issues. We are eager to consider original scholarship, including broadly based histories of both long-standing and more recent immigrant populations; focused investigations of ethnic enclaves and understudied subgroups; and examinations of relationships among various cultural, regional, and socioeconomic communities. We also welcome manuscripts on subject areas that need further critical inquiry, including the social and economic impacts of coronavirus (COVID-19), transnationalism, globalization, homeland polity, and other pertinent topics.

Chasing the American Dream in China

~

Chinese Americans
in the Ancestral Homeland

LESLIE KIM WANG

Rutgers University Press

New Brunswick, Camden, and Newark, New Jersey, and London

Library of Congress Cataloging-in-Publication Data

Names: Wang, Leslie K., author.
Title: Chasing the American dream in China : Chinese Americans
in the ancestral homeland / Leslie K. Wang.
Other titles: Chinese Americans in the ancestral homeland
Description: New Brunswick : Rutgers University Press, 2021. | Series: Asian
American studies today | Includes bibliographical references and index.
Identifiers: LCCN 2020031070 | ISBN 9780813599366 (paperback) |
ISBN 9780813599373 (hardcover) | ISBN 9780813599380 (epub) |
ISBN 9780813599397 (mobi) | ISBN 9780813599403 (pdf)
Subjects: LCSH: Chinese Americans—China. | Chinese Americans—
Ethnic identity. | China—Emigration and immigration. | Americans—
China—Social conditions. | Immigrants—China—Social conditions. |
American Dream.
Classification: LCC DS731.A54 W36 2021 | DDC 951/.004951073—dc23
LC record available at https://lccn.loc.gov/2020031070

A British Cataloging-in-Publication record for this book is available
from the British Library.

♾ The paper used in this publication meets the requirements of the American
National Standard for Information Sciences—Permanence of Paper for Printed
Library Materials, ANSI Z39.48-1992.

www.rutgersuniversitypress.org

Manufactured in the United States of America

For Dino and Theo,
who light up my life

Contents

Chasing the American Dream in China

1

Introduction

In 1997 I decided to spend my junior year of college studying abroad in Beijing, the capital of the People's Republic of China (PRC). The application required letters of recommendation from university instructors. I met in office hours with Matt,[1] a gaunt mid-thirtyish white graduate student who was a teaching assistant in one of my classes. With his brow furrowed, he asked me, "Are you *sure* you want to go to China? There's a lot of restrictions on freedom and rights there." Taken aback, I described my desire to spend an entire year in my parents' country of birth—a place I had never even visited. I would spend the summer taking classes at Tsinghua University—known as China's MIT—then move for the academic year to Peking University—known as China's Harvard. But more personally, I had been raised in 1980s America, an era that emphasized cultural assimilation to white mainstream society. In going to China, I sought to improve my Mandarin skills and connect with my long-lost origins. I also hoped to locate a sense of emotional belonging in China that had never seemed fully available to me in the United States. Matt begrudgingly agreed to write the letter.

Undeterred, I arrived in Beijing on a stiflingly hot, muggy June day. Stepping out of the airport and into the throngs of people, I was overwhelmed by noise and chaos. Chain-smoking hawkers and taxi drivers milled around, aggressively bombarding weary travelers with offers of car rides and hotel deals. To stay cool, middle-aged men wore translucent white-cotton tank tops rolled up to their armpits, exposing their stomachs to the humid air. I soon located the sixty other students in my study abroad program, who, like me, were mostly American-born Chinese (ABCs) from California. Busses transported us across the vast metropolis of Beijing, which at that time had only two simple subway lines, compared to the twenty-three that crisscross the city today. The other students chatted with excitement as I gazed in a jet-lagged stupor at the colorful street signs written in unrecognizable characters. As the bus weaved its way around city workers who were setting fire to piles of trash in the middle of the road, doubts began to creep into my mind. "What have I gotten myself into?" I wondered.

Adjusting to life in Beijing took time. I did not fit in. Just like many others who "return" to their ancestral homeland in search of cultural belonging, I was surprised to find that I had never felt more foreign nor more American. My extremely limited knowledge of East Asian history compounded my discomfort. Two weeks after arriving, Hong Kong reverted back to mainland Chinese rule after ninety-nine years of British sovereignty. A group of us gathered around a tiny dorm-room television to watch the formal handover ceremony. I had no idea what was happening. Seeing my confusion, a Singaporean Chinese classmate patiently explained the significance of the occasion to me.

Interacting with locals was challenging due to a combination of my inadequate language skills and their very high expectations of me as a Chinese descendant. During my first long train ride—a twelve-hour journey to Nanjing—a married couple in their thirties, both doctors, occupied the beds opposite from me. Upon finding out I was an ABC (the first they had ever met), the woman peppered me with questions about my family history and tested my knowledge of Chinese holidays and traditions. Equipped with only a childlike vocabulary, I could not find the words to answer her with any semblance of intelligence. Her disappointment was palpable. She leaned back against the wall and folded her arms over her chest judgmentally, muttering under her breath that I had lost touch with my roots.

Seemingly on a daily basis, whenever I climbed into a taxi my broken Chinese invariably caused the curious driver to swivel around and inquire in a strong Beijing drawl, "Nali lai de?" (Where are you from?). At first I tried to explain that I was from the United States. However, this nearly always elicited the same incredulous reply, "But you don't look American!" It soon became apparent that to local people, "American" (*meiguoren*) was equivalent to a white person with blond hair and blue eyes. Changing tactics, I began to describe myself as Chinese American (*meiji huaren*). This approach was more time-consuming, as it required recounting my parents' migration histories. Although both were born in China, my mother moved to the United States in the late 1950s as the child of an educational migrant. Meanwhile, my father's family fled to Taiwan— along with roughly two million others—to escape the Chinese Communist takeover of the PRC in 1949. He met my mother after moving to Colorado in the mid-1960s to pursue a PhD in engineering. Eventually, they settled in Southern California, where I was born and raised. As the months of study abroad passed, I grew tired of this recitation. To avoid it, I finally began claiming to be Korean—the most populous foreign group in China, with a large contingent of students studying in Beijing's universities.[2] This generally provoked no further questions and ensured a peaceful ride.

Despite feeling out of place, I enjoyed an unprecedented sense of freedom in Beijing that stemmed from my physical similarities to the locals. Walking down the street, riding my bike, or taking the crowded subway, I experienced the tranquil anonymity that comes with blending in with the ethnic majority. My reference point began drifting away from the United States and toward East Asia. Having grown up with the implicit feeling that my Chinese ancestry was something to be downplayed, or even ashamed of, I reveled being in an environment where everyone—including pop stars and celebrities—had Asian features. As long as I did not open my mouth, the locals assumed that I was native Chinese. On multiple occasions, the brusque door monitor of my building refused to let me enter, accusing me of trying to sneak into the foreign dorms.

At the same time, I remained keenly aware of my American citizenship and used it to my advantage whenever possible, such as during another long train ride. Unable to reserve seats, my friends and I were stuck in the drafty, deafeningly loud space between two clanging cars. Managing to locate a train conductor, we pulled out our passports. He scanned the photos and glanced back up at our faces several times, perplexed. "We're Chinese American!" we implored pitifully. Minutes later, he escorted us past hundreds of locals, who were tightly jammed into hard, uncomfortable upright seats, and gave us expensive sleeper bunks.

After a full year abroad I returned to San Diego, which, compared to the dynamism of Beijing, seemed staid and boring. Living abroad had expanded my worldview and instilled a deep and abiding curiosity about my ancestral homeland. Yet China remained a puzzling enigma; the more language, culture, and history I learned, the less I seemed to understand. Was China my emotional homeland? What did it mean to be "authentically" Chinese? And how did my changing relationship with my parents' birth country affect my American identity? I decided to pursue an academic path to investigate these issues.

Nearly a decade passed before I lived in the PRC again on a long-term basis, when I returned as a twenty-nine-year-old PhD candidate to conduct a year of intensive dissertation fieldwork. I marveled at the massive transformation the country had undergone during the years I'd been away. My nostalgic memories of eating dumplings in shabby, hole-in-the-wall restaurants; taking illegal yellow *mian di* (bread loaf–shaped) taxis; and seeing no other foreigners on the streets were outdated, packaged neatly in my mind like a time capsule of the late-1990s.

Instead, the city had become a prime destination for young Western expatriates searching for opportunities and adventure. It was also modernizing at lightning speed. Centuries-old *hutong*—long, narrow neighborhoods of traditional courtyard homes—were being torn down and hastily replaced with gleaming subway lines, glass and steel high-rises, and miles of new expressways as the city prepared for the 2008 Summer Olympics, an event meant to solidify the nation's status as a global superpower. Daily news headlines shouted warnings that the United States and China were beginning to face off in a fierce economic competition.

I, too, had changed in the intervening years, and my reasons for engaging with China had also shifted. Compared with my study abroad experience, during which I sought to connect with culture through language learning and travel, my second visit was markedly different. Nearing thirty, I was less preoccupied with fitting in and more focused on my professional path. Although I had vastly improved my language skills and had more solid grounding in Chinese history and culture, I no longer expected to share an innate sense of belonging with the locals. This time, I was on a mission to launch my career.

Others, however, continued to define me as Chinese. One morning, I took a taxi to a research site outside Beijing. I recounted my background to the driver, an amiable working-class man in his mid-fifties. "Ni hui dao Zhongguo le!" (You came back to China!), he remarked approvingly. Catching my eye in the rearview mirror, he then asked somberly, "If China and the United States ever went to war, which country would you support?" Caught off guard, I stammered awkwardly that I did not believe in war. "You should always support China," the driver lectured me sternly, "because it's your *zuguo* [motherland]!" Later, I repeated the driver's question to a group of white Americans. I waited for them to scoff, since it seemed so obvious to me which country I would support. Instead, the conversation stopped. A young blond man broke the silence, tentatively posing the question no one else knew how to ask: "So, how did you answer?"

What does it mean to be Chinese American in an increasingly transnational era? These autobiographical stories barely scratch the surface when it comes to the complex nature of racial, ethnic, and cultural belonging for second-generation ABCs whose lives span across borders.[3] This book draws from interviews conducted between 2013 and 2018 with sixty Chinese American professionals who worked on a long-term basis in the global cities of Beijing and

Shanghai. These children of immigrants occupy an undefined space. Situated between countries and cultures, their bridging of boundaries can be either empowering or disempowering, depending on the social context they are in. This book examines how ABCs—highly skilled first-world migrants to an ancestral homeland that also happens to be the second most powerful economy in the world—strategically used their in-betweenness to gain personal advantage in China.

Compared to other immigrant groups in the United States, Chinese Americans generally occupy a privileged status with regard to income, educational attainment, and integration into mainstream society.[4] This is certainly true of the individuals featured in this study; all but one had earned a U.S. bachelor's degree and nearly half had obtained a master's degree or higher. Nonetheless, they chose to exchange comfortable lives for unpredictable futures in the PRC. This decision is intriguing given that most Americans view the country unfavorably, suspicious of its authoritarian political system and fearful of its growing economic and technological prowess.[5] Furthermore, despite the nation's rapid development and expanding global influence, the PRC still qualifies as a developing country, in which issues such as food safety, overcrowding, and hazardous levels of air, soil, and water pollution dramatically affect the overall quality of life. These issues have pushed millions of Chinese citizens *out* of the country and into the industrialized global North.

This paradox raises a number of questions that underlie this study, the first in-depth analysis of Chinese American ancestral homeland migration. Why do highly skilled ABCs who could ostensibly do quite well in the U.S. economy choose to relocate to China during their prime career-building years? In what ways do they feel as if they are "returning" to an emotional homeland? By extension, how is their sense of racial and ethnic identity altered, challenged, or reinforced through living there? And finally, considering the PRC's vastly different history and context of gender relations, how do the experiences of Chinese American women and men compare?

As racialized minorities in the United States, Chinese Americans are often perceived and treated as perennial foreigners. Upon moving to the PRC, however, they are granted automatic membership into the dominant racial and ethnic group. Here it is important to distinguish between race and ethnicity. Race is a system of power governed by the dominant group, which "draws on physical differences to construct and give meaning to racial boundaries and the hierarchy of which they are a part"; by contrast, ethnicity is characterized by a "self-conscious sense of group membership" based on perceptions of common ancestry, history, symbols, and traditions.[6] In China, race, ethnicity, and cultural belonging are generally understood to be the outcomes of blood ties. Regardless of nationality or birthplace, those with Chinese ancestry are seen as having an intrinsic, primordial connection to the country.[7] At the same time, separated from their ethnic homeland by time, geography, and cultural and political socialization, ABCs lack a guaranteed emotional connection to their new environment. These factors raise complex questions about how identity and belonging are constructed and experienced within transnational settings.

The research in this book reveals that "returning" to an ancestral homeland is neither simple nor straightforward. Contrary to assumptions, it is not a direct path to achieving emotional belonging. Instead, I contend that regardless of whether they are in the United States or China, ABCs are denied recognition and acknowledgment of the rich, nuanced, and fundamentally in-between nature of their lived experiences. This is because they straddle overly simplistic dichotomies of American versus Chinese, foreigner versus native, and insider versus outsider. Yet my interviews reveal that rather than being constrained by essentialistic binaries, these high-skilled elite professionals consciously maneuvered between simplistic assumptions about their racial, ethnic, and cultural backgrounds to propel themselves further in the Chinese economy. During a time of unprecedented shifts in the global economic order, these unique first-world migrants have strategically used their in-betweenness to pursue the American Dream abroad.

Prior to 1978, when the PRC began transitioning to a capitalist market economy, it was unthinkable that a Westerner might pursue a professional path there. As the nation began the process of reform and opening up (known as *gaige kaifang*) after decades of economic, social, and political isolation from the outside world, the Chinese government created a powerful, if seemingly contradictory, system that has combined capitalist economic practices with an authoritarian political regime. The results have been nothing short of remarkable.

Between 1989 and 2018, the PRC's annual GDP skyrocketed by an average of nearly 10 percent annually.[8] As the country has transformed into a hub of global manufacturing and consumption, roughly *eight hundred million* people have been pulled above the poverty line, with China's growth accounting for three-quarters of all global poverty reduction since 1980.[9] Life expectancy rates in the PRC have shot up, children are far out-earning their parents, and the Chinese rank far higher than Americans in optimism, a key economic indicator. For the first time in history, there are more billionaires in Asia than in the United States.[10] A 2018 *New York Times* headline sums it up: "The American Dream Is Alive. In China."[11]

Much of China's success is attributable to international trade, particularly with the United States. Although each is the other's largest trading partner, the two countries maintain a volatile relationship. The American media—especially right-wing outlets—has tended to portray the PRC as an aggressive foreign menace that seeks to dominate or even destabilize the free world. The isolationist rhetoric and policies of the Trump administration, as well as a protracted trade war instituted in 2018 and the coronavirus pandemic of 2020, have undoubtedly exacerbated these issues. Even so, this characterization of East Asians as a "yellow peril" long predates the current period. First popularized in the late nineteenth and early twentieth centuries, Asian immigrants have often been regarded as a menace "to American identity as the country of the

White race and Western civilization."[12] The current regime, led by President Xi Jinping, is often lumped together with Russia and North Korea as the world's primary threats to democratic values.

At the same time, fueled largely by China's more open global stance, Asians have become the fastest-growing racial or ethnic group in the United States.[13] Over two million Chinese people from the PRC, Taiwan, Hong Kong, and Macau constitute both the largest Asian group and the largest immigrant group of *any* origin in the country.[14] Since economic reforms began, millions of PRC citizens have moved to the United States to study, work, and live on a long-term basis or settle down permanently.

Scholars looking at these trends have typically focused on the incorporation and assimilation of Chinese people into American society. On the other hand, few studies have considered how the forces of global capitalism and free trade have also inspired migration in the *opposite* direction, attracting thousands of twenty- and thirtysomething Westerners, including ABCs, to China's global cities. The last official Chinese census in 2010 reported the number of U.S. citizens residing there at 71,493 (excluding study abroad students).[15] Because Chinese Americans are counted as part of the total number of Americans in the country, there are no definitive statistics. Nonetheless, they are an integral group within affluent Western expatriate communities, whose "comparatively small numbers contrast with their disproportionally significant role in global capitalism."[16]

ABC professionals have found themselves uniquely poised to serve as cultural liaisons and facilitators of relations between the world's two most powerful adversaries. Having Chinese heritage can take on positive cultural meanings in the ethnic motherland as it becomes "the source of something immutable that does not fade over generations and creates a sense of community and connection back to the country from which their parents and/or grandparents emigrated."[17] Hence, despite the fears of China as a growing yellow peril, for the past few decades the country has also loomed large in the American imagination as a place of untold economic possibility.

Forever Foreign in the United States, Perpetually Chinese in China

The U.S. Immigration and Nationality Act of 1965 marked a major turning point in which immigrants from Latin America and East Asia began to outnumber those from Europe. The law dismantled prior quotas and prioritized skilled migration and family reunification regardless of national origin, opening the door to a wave of educational and professional migrants. Post-1965 East Asian migrants and their children have been associated with "positive" racial and ethnic stereotypes, labeled model minorities whose success is "attributed to stronger values emphasizing hard work, achievement, and belief in the American dream."[18] Indeed, as Yoo and colleagues have argued, "This characterization of individual efforts and mobility justifies the assertion that anyone can make significant achievements as long as they work hard, and those who do not have only themselves to blame."[19]

The deceptive label of the model minority has pitted people of color and racialized immigrant groups against one another in ways that reinforce white privilege, as being deigned exemplary minorities creates both envy and resentment in other groups.[20] The commonplace lumping together of all Asian American populations also obscures the major socioeconomic differences that exist between and within various subpopulations. According to a recent Pew Research Center study, income inequality is now greatest among Asian Americans. In 2016, the wealthiest Asians in the United States had incomes nearly eleven times higher than those who earned the least.[21] Hence, the uniform stereotype of Asian Americans as highly educated white-collar professionals renders invisible large groups of working-class and poor migrants who reside in ethnic enclaves. In cities such as New York, where up to one-quarter of Chinese Americans live in poverty, many lack legal status as they work long hours in restaurants and other service occupations.[22]

The model minority myth also disguises persistent anti-Asian sentiment in American society,[23] in which racism and prejudice is interpreted through the more limited lens of Black-white relations. Psychological experiments have shown implicit bias against Asians, who are considered high in competence but low in sociability/likability.[24] As a result of being associated with foreignness due to perceived racial and cultural differences from the white mainstream, ABCs have difficulty being recognized as "real" Americans (recall that my classmates genuinely wanted to know, in a hypothetical war between the United States and China, which I would support). Asian people in the United States thus continually grapple with issues of belonging. "Assumptions that one is not a citizen, does not speak English well, or insinuations that one should 'go back to China' (even if one has never been there)," writes Andrea Louie, "constitute a set of racist behaviors that frame perceptions of all Chinese Americans as perpetually foreign and 'other' to mainstream U.S. society."[25]

By mere happenstance, on the other side of the Pacific, China's enthusiastic embrace of global capitalism created unprecedented opportunities for highly skilled ABCs to become key players within expanding financial sectors. There they grapple with the pressures to conform based on inclusive assumptions of racial and ethnic belonging. Although a well-established body of scholarship has shown that Chinese Americans in the United States are treated as perpetual foreigners,[26] few have examined whether the inverse holds true for ABCs in the ancestral homeland, where they are considered *perpetually Chinese*, regardless of how long their families have been settled abroad. Put another way, ABCs' social exclusion in the United States is based on essentialized racial and ethnic differences, while in the PRC, ABCs are included in the dominant group based on essentialized racial and ethnic sameness.

Consider Kimberly Chen, an articulate twenty-three-year-old woman who had been working as an HR manager in Beijing for two years when we met. Her parents grew up in Ningbo, near Shanghai, before moving to Southern California in the early 1990s and raising children there. Kimberly had earned an accelerated bachelor's degree at UC Berkeley, forgoing the chance to study abroad.

Wanting to improve her Mandarin and experience cultural immersion, Kimberly moved to Beijing directly after graduation. With a mix of humor and exasperation, she recounted the diverse strategies she used for identifying her ethnicity and cultural background to local people. Like I had years before, Kimberly had grown tired of constantly being asked about her origins by inquisitive Chinese co-workers, cab drivers, and random strangers. "It depends on who asks me!" she sighed with resignation. "Sometimes I don't care to tell people the truth. It takes too long to explain."

Kimberly experimented with different approaches over the years, which led to different outcomes. When she told people that her family was from Ningbo (a city with its own dialect), they assumed she was also a mainlander who spoke accented Mandarin. Others heard her less-than-perfect language skills and wondered whether she was South Korean. "Sometimes I'll actually just lie and say I'm Korean so I don't have to explain things to them," the young woman admitted. Only occasionally would she identify herself as Chinese American, knowing it would inspire a lengthy— but by now predictable—discussion about her decision to "return." Kimberly remarked, "People are interested in knowing why I came back to China. Everyone is always very curious, 'Xiang hui dao Zhongguo?' [You wanted to return to China?], and I'm like, I didn't 'hui dao Zhongguo' [return to China]. I came here pretty much for the first time, and I didn't know what it was like before."

The lack of clarity about Kimberly's ethnic identity emerged from a localized set of assumptions about what it means to be Chinese. Depending on context, China can be defined as "a geographic entity, a nation, a government, a people or race, [or] a culture."[27] Unless ABCs speak completely unaccented Mandarin (a rare and difficult feat), locals nearly always ask where they are from. When asked in the United States, this question inquires about one's country of origin. In the PRC, however, it refers to one's *laojia*, or ancestral village. As L. Ling-chi Wang explains, Chinese identity is "inextricably tied to and equated with one's ancestral village. The bond to one's roots is [considered] unique, sacred, and eternal."[28]

Because China is considered the center of authenticity for the entire diaspora, overseas descendants (known as *huaren*) are expected to carry an innate sense of belonging and identification with their ethnic heritage, even if they are many generations removed. Thus, hyphenated cultural identities are unintelligible to local people, who consider ABCs to be Chinese people who happen to hold American citizenship. Whether they are in the United States or in the ancestral homeland, ABCs are understood—or misunderstood—in similar ways.

Performing Flexible Identities in China

When Elizabeth Wu's husband was offered a lucrative managerial position in Shanghai, the thirty-seven-year-old mother of two relocated her life and family. She possessed a bachelor's degree from Stanford University, a master's degree from Harvard, and high-level Mandarin skills. When we spoke, the self-identified Taiwanese American woman projected an air of competence while discussing her work as a health-care consultant for a multinational corporation that partnered with Chinese state authorities. Elizabeth, who had lived in China for three years, let me in on a secret: she strategically claimed membership in different ethnic or nationality groups depending on the context and desired outcome. She lightheartedly described this versatility: "If you need me to be Taiwanese, I'll be Taiwanese. If you need me to be Chinese, I'll be Chinese. If you need me to play American, I'll be American. You sort of switch." But at the end of the day, she mused, "I'm more American than anything."

Scholars argue that rather than being a primordial trait, ethnicity is in fact a performance that emerges from social interaction. According to Joanne Nagel, "The individual carries a portfolio of ethnic identities that are more or less salient in various situations and vis-à-vis various audiences. As audiences change, the socially-defined array of ethnic choices open to the individual changes."[29] Furthermore, individuals can exert agency during these performances to maximize their personal gain. From this perspective, ethnic identity is "merely 'a thing' subject to manipulation and differential presentation" rather than "a reflection of the true self."[30]

Elizabeth was just one of many respondents who viewed her identity as flexible by consciously portraying herself as an insider to diverse audiences. The highly skilled ABCs I met in Beijing and Shanghai leveraged their elite global status, which was made more powerful in conjunction with local assumptions about their emotional ties to the motherland and inborn cultural understanding (considered unattainable by non-Chinese). In this book, I refer to this ability to shift between distinct categories of belonging to create personal social and economic advantage as "strategic in-betweenness."[31] As Western economic migrants with American educational backgrounds, vast amounts of cultural capital, and English-language fluency, my participants benefited far more from their in-betweenness than do the more numerous ancestral homeland migrants who move from lesser developed to more industrialized countries.[32]

In China, blood-based notions of belonging also bring a host of cultural expectations—such as having fluent Mandarin skills and immense cultural knowledge—that ABCs must learn to skillfully negotiate if they want to be successful there. Nonetheless, their inclusion within the dominant social category permits new kinds of freedom, allowing them to creatively switch among identities to further their own interests. As influential liaisons, my respondents have played a large role in introducing first-world tastes, ideas, practices, and goods to millions of newly middle-class Chinese consumers. Rather than accomplishing this through "flexible citizenship,"[33] in which Asian elites establish citizenship in different countries as an economic strategy, the ABCs I interviewed used strategic in-betweenness—the flexibility of which has created very favorable professional outcomes for both women and men, including rapid career growth and enhanced opportunities. In the social sphere, however, the outcomes differed by gender. I found that heterosexual men gained access to a diverse array of local dating and marriage possibilities that vastly outweighed their options back home—a situation that was not shared by their female Chinese American peers.

The skilled migrants in this study thus deliberately maneuvered between countries, cultures, and ascribed identity categories to further their careers and maximize opportunities in the swiftly changing global economy—one in which China's power and influence has been predicted to soon surpass that of the United States. Although there is a well-developed literature on the malleability of racial and ethnic identity in the United States,[34] this phenomenon has not been thoroughly examined among co-ethnic transnational migrants. The process by which ABC professionals play with categories of belonging in the ancestral homeland highlights ethnic identity as "a dynamic outcome of complex social relations that operate at multiple levels within a globalized world."[35]

Second-Generation Ancestral Homeland Migration

The stories highlighted in this book challenge earlier paradigmatic understandings of international migration as a process in which newcomers would gradually embrace the language, values, and norms of their host society and leave their origins behind. For centuries, however, migrants have maintained deep socioeconomic ties with their home countries.[36] Recent innovations in technology and transportation have rapidly increased the circulation of people, money, ideas, and practices across borders. This has occurred through transnationalism, which has been defined as "the processes by which immigrants build social fields that link together their country of origin and their country of settlement."[37]

Today, migration is a circular process for many immigrants who choose to resettle in their home countries or move back and forth between home and host societies—a trend known as "strategic switching." David Ley and Audrey Kobayashi, who studied the migration patterns of Chinese Canadians, found that many first-generation migrants relocated between Hong Kong and Vancouver at different life stages as their priorities changed from obtaining education to building their careers to enjoying a higher quality of life in retirement. Their Western-born children have emulated these patterns.[38]

Until now, the field of transnationalism has tended to emphasize the experiences of first-generation returnees and been sluggish in acknowledging the transnational behavior of the second generation.[39] Nonetheless, a handful of studies have examined second- and later-generation co-ethnic return to the PRC. Typically focused on short homeland trips taken by Chinese American tourists inspired by the desire to connect with their ancestral origins, a common theme of these studies is the unexpected sense of dislocation they experience; this differs greatly from their expectations of feeling a sense of cultural belonging during their travels.[40]

Andrea Louie examined the experiences of later-generation ABCs who visited their ancestral villages in Guangdong Province on Chinese state-organized homeland tours in the late 1990s. While these trips sought to promote emotional belonging to the motherland, she found that participants' deeper understanding of Chinese culture and ancestral origins as a result of these return visits actually "legitimize[d] their identities" as Asian Americans in the United States.[41] Unlike the people featured in this book, Louie's subjects had overtly affective reasons for visiting, and their short-term stays were not motivated by financial reasons. Furthermore, she conducted this research before China became an economic juggernaut.

Nazli Kibria interviewed second-generation Chinese American "roots" tourists and found that they were automatically granted societal membership in the PRC based on blood ties and ancestry. At the same time, they experienced weaker than expected emotional attachment upon realizing that their different societal outlooks and lack of language ability excluded them from true national belonging. Still, these young people recognized that building cultural ties to their ethnic homeland could create potential financial benefits for them in the future.[42]

Homeland trips can create profound discomfort and ambivalence when roots tourists stay for only a short time. A permanent or semipermanent move is a different story. Second-generation ABC professionals who immerse themselves in Chinese society on a long-term basis possess dramatically different objectives and achieve different outcomes that stem from their ability to use strategic in-betweenness. For them, maneuvering between ascribed categories of belonging serves as an empowering form of social capital that distinguishes them from both locals and other expatriates.

Chinese Incentives to Attract Western Talent

Rapid Chinese economic expansion, combined with slowing growth in many Western first-world countries, has attracted many first-world workers to the PRC's global cities; indeed, the first decade of the twenty-first century saw a 35 percent increase in the number of foreign residents.[43] Even so, the PRC does not offer incentives—such as dual citizenship—to garner the interest and investment of overseas Chinese.[44] Instead, Chinese leaders, who "have long considered Chinese abroad to be sojourners who retain ties and loyalty to China, part of a belief that 'once a Chinese always a Chinese,'" have focused their efforts on attracting highly skilled American-trained Chinese-born professionals.[45] Conse-quently, official policies regarding overseas Chinese typically "seek to gain the return and investments of ethnic Chinese who are still nationals."[46]

Here it's important to clarify Chinese governmental distinc-tions between categories of people with Chinese ancestry. *Zhong-guoren* refers to native-born Chinese citizens. In terms of overseas Chinese, *huayi* or *huaren* refers to diasporic Chinese who are born and raised abroad. Official policies distinguish them from *hua-qiao*: PRC-born individuals who moved abroad later and typically retain Chinese citizenship. It is this last group that the Chinese government has focused on attracting back. Although American-born Chinese (*meiji huaren*) are counted as Chinese in light of common ancestry and shared cultural background, they are not trusted as having the same "obligations and loyalties of political affiliation" to the nation as *zhongguoren*.[47]

Since the 1990s, PRC authorities have established numerous special economic development zones aimed at luring back *huaqiao* professionals to build the local knowledge economy. In 2008, the government created the Thousand Talents Program, offering financial and social incentives to thousands of elite Western-trained Chinese scientists in the hope of expanding a range of high-tech industries.[48] Individuals are selected for their "transnational cultural capital," defined by Na Ren and Hong Liu as "education, intellect, knowledge, skills, mindset, networks, and other cultural experiences, which are transferable and portable across national boundaries."[49] Government investment in these fields has been staggering. In 2017, the country spent 1.76 trillion yuan ($254 billion) on research and development in genetic technologies alone.

In comparison, the lack of interest in recruiting high-skilled members of the Western diaspora reveals clear distinctions between the generalized social membership offered to all descendants and the furthering of specific national objectives entrusted only to those who are Chinese born. This may relate to the exponential rates of voluntary permanent return among native Chinese who have obtained first-world educational and professional experience.[50] Over the past forty years, more than 5 million Chinese students have gone abroad, and over 3.1 million have returned.[51] Known as *haigui* (meaning "overseas returnee" or "sea turtle"), their numbers soared alongside the dual phenomena of the PRC's massive growth and the 2008 global recession. Nowadays, roughly 80 percent of Chinese students choose to return after completing their overseas studies, compared to only one-third of students in 2006.[52]

In these ways, China is distinguishable from other Asian countries, which offer attractive incentives to strengthen ties with Western diasporic groups. For example, the Vietnamese government guarantees overseas Vietnamese five-year visa exemptions and dual citizenship for themselves, spouses, and children.[53] The Indian government grants lifelong multiple-entry, multipurpose visas to those who can prove Indian ancestry up to the fourth generation.[54] Japan has a special renewable visa for foreign nationals up to the third generation (provided at least one grandparent was a Japanese national), allowing individuals to legally reside in the country for three to five years and to move between jobs.[55] Furthermore, overseas Koreans from industrialized countries enjoy a special visa status that grants quasi-citizenship rights, including the right to work, prolonged residence, medical care, and property ownership in South Korea.[56] The relative absence of Chinese state policies tying the country to Western diasporic populations makes the reverse migration of ABCs a more self-directed and entrepreneurial endeavor.

Participants and Methods

This book is based on sixty in-depth qualitative interviews with second-generation Chinese American professionals (half women, half men) conducted in Beijing and Shanghai during the summers of 2013, 2014, and 2018.[57] These two cities are centers of trade and knowledge production and feature large, thriving expatriate communities.[58] Participants ranged in age from twenty-two to forty-six, with a mean age of thirty-two. They had spent an average of nearly five years working in China, with the majority relocating during their mid- to late twenties. At the time of interview, seventeen participants were married, four were engaged, and three were divorced. Eight were parents of at least one child. My sample also included one single woman who does not adhere to sexual labels and two single female and one male partnered LGBT+ participants; the women chose not to reveal their sexual orientations publicly due to the perceived lack of social acceptance for same-sex partnerships and queer lifestyles in China.[59] (See table A.1.)

Significantly, even though everyone self-identified as Chinese American, over 70 percent ($n = 40$) had parental connections to Taiwan. In brief, the Taiwanese can be divided into three separate groups with Chinese ancestry: the long-settled Fujianese and Cantonese, and the more newly arrived mainland Chinese. Referred to as *waishengren*, meaning "people from other provinces," the latter group was affiliated with the Kuomintang Party (KMT), which lost the civil war against the Chinese Communists in 1949.[60] During the mid- to late 1940s, a mass exodus of two million KMT affiliates left for neighboring Taiwan. The KMT subsequently took over power and remains the major political party on the island.

Taiwan's political status is a controversial and unresolved issue, with Taiwan claiming independent statehood and the PRC claiming it as part of its territory.[61] Furthermore, many *waishengren* in the United States continue to deeply identify with Chinese culture and espouse a pro-China political stance. Consequently, the ethnic identification of second-generation Taiwanese Americans tends to be quite flexible, allowing them to claim membership as either Taiwanese American or Chinese American depending on the context.[62] As one twenty-nine-year-old man who spent his early years in Taiwan explained to me, "I consider myself Chinese in the *broader* sense of what it means to be Chinese."

Because the Chinese government's isolationist policies mostly forbade migration until the late 1970s, American authorities allowed Taiwan to fulfill the PRC's immigration quotas. With comparatively high levels of education upon arrival, these Taiwanese immigrants achieved quite successful outcomes compared to native-born Americans or other immigrant populations. Today, Taiwanese immigrants are twice as likely to earn a U.S. bachelor's degree and three times as likely to attain an advanced degree than immigrants overall. That elevated level of education correlates to higher annual incomes, health insurance coverage, homeownership rates, and naturalization rates—advantages that have been passed down to their children.[63]

Even when compared to other Chinese Americans, the educational attainment of my participants was remarkably high. Nearly everyone received a bachelor's degree from an American university (one person—a professional chef/restaurateur—did not attend college). Moreover, almost half ($n = 29$) had earned an advanced degree before moving to China. This correlated with their parents' educational attainment, with twenty-six having at least one parent who had earned an American master's degree or PhD. Most participants had also gained several years of U.S. work experience before leaving for China.

Nearly everyone worked in four main areas: (1) as entrepreneurs, with their own restaurants, bars, shops, or companies; (2) in education and research; (3) in arts and media; or (4) as corporate managers or directors in multinational or expatriate-run companies. Only two worked in the nonprofit field, and none were full-time volunteers. The fact that all worked for pay, and mostly in white-collar positions, distinguished them from expats who move to China to engage in humanitarian efforts.[64] Furthermore, I purposely chose not to interview anyone who was employed as an English teacher—highly transient work that is generally disparaged as low status, low skilled, and low paid. Thus, these ABCs had a very different experience than their Asian American co-ethnic "returnee" peers in other East Asian countries, such as Japan and South Korea, who work indefinitely as English teachers and face challenges obtaining jobs with the potential for upward advancement.[65]

My respondents' ability to serve as cultural liaisons definitely depended on their possession of adequate language skills. Everyone reported having at least an intermediate level of Mandarin competency, although roughly one-quarter learned the language as adults after being raised in English or Cantonese-speaking households. The vast majority viewed their time in the PRC as a temporary career-building stage in which they could amass skills that would be transferable to the American or other Western industrialized context. Working in the ancestral homeland was generally part of their broader life plan, with roughly 85 percent aiming to eventually move back to the United States to raise children or enjoy a higher quality of life. It's also important to note that I only interviewed individuals whose parents were both Chinese; thus, this book does not include the perspectives of people who are mixed race, as their experiences differ so greatly.

A NOTE ON TERMINOLOGY

There is no consensus on terms that refer to second-generation co-ethnic migrants to parental homelands. Many phrases that are used interchangeably—such as "return migrants," "diasporic return migrants," and "ancestral return migrants"—overlook the fact that these individuals have not actually returned to their country of origin. They also tend to lump first- and second-generation migrants together into one group. Jane Yamashiro argues that this is problematic because it "assumes that co-ethnics go to the ancestral homeland because of ethnic ties, which does not always coincide with the actual experiences or identification of migrants."[66] To avoid these issues, this analysis employs Yamashiro's more inclusive term "ancestral homeland migrants."[67]

I also do not refer to my participants as expatriates, because they generally did not identify as such. Like many other first-world citizens who move to developing regions, most consciously distanced themselves from this term: one that is "socially contested, politically and morally charged" as well as historically associated with a white, upper-class, colonial lifestyle.[68] Even though the ABCs I interviewed primarily socialized in Western circles, they tended to define expatriates as white corporate executives brought to China on expensive "expat packages." My subjects continually defined themselves *against* white foreigners, drawing on their shared cultural and ethnic characteristics with locals to place themselves somewhere between native Chinese and expatriates. Finally, all respondents in this book are referred to as ABCs, even if they were born abroad and technically qualify as members of the 1.5 generation. Everyone referred to themselves as ABCs, since they were primarily raised, educated, and socialized in the United States.

The Chapters to Follow

This study tells the stories of individuals who are redefining what it means to be both Chinese and American in a transnational age. Examining their experiences in the ancestral homeland provides a unique lens through which to view the multifaceted, performative nature of racial and ethnic identity and belonging and how these are shaped by larger social, economic, and geopolitical forces. As educated middle-class Western sojourners who choose to migrate— rather than being forced or compelled by reasons of survival to leave their home country—ABCs' elevated global social status provides them with opportunities unattainable to the average local Chinese citizen. They act as indispensable liaisons, strengthening cooperative ties between economic superpowers locked in a battle for global dominance, even as they find themselves in competition with large numbers of increasingly skilled Western-trained *haigui* returnees.

Chapter 2 examines the significance of transnational ties between ABCs and the ancestral homeland while growing up, focusing on how they develop cultural belonging and ethnic identity in accordance with their experiences of racism, discrimination, and being labeled a "model minority" in the United States. I also discuss their early homeland journeys, including family return trips taken during childhood, as opposed to college study abroad experiences and independent travel that they chose to undertake to China. While family trips were characterized in terms of familial obligation and thus held little personal meaning, their later travels to the ancestral homeland were primarily motivated by emotional reasons. In particular, the transnational practices they engaged in as young adults were often prompted by the desire to resolve identity-based issues and feelings of marginalization in mainstream American society.

Chapter 3 explores ABCs' motivations for moving to the ancestral homeland during their career-building years and how they used their ambiguous social status to create unique professional advantages within China's growing economy. Scholars have argued that Asian Americans cannot assert ethnic identities at will in the United States due to their ascribed status as racialized minorities.[69] However, ABCs' phenotypical similarities to mainland Chinese, combined with their Western backgrounds and skill sets, allowed them to move flexibly between a range of ethnic options. Within the context of global capitalism, ethnic ambiguity became a form of social capital that they used to maximize their economic and social advantage.

Chapter 4 explores the potential drawbacks of strategic in-betweenness. I argue that due to simplistic assumptions about blood ties, ethnicity, race, and nationality in China, the category of "ABC" is not seen as a meaningful or legitimate identity. Despite enjoying myriad benefits of in-betweenness both in and outside the workplace, respondents were also expected by local people to competently perform Chineseness. These difficult-to-meet expectations included possessing high levels of Mandarin language fluency, having a nuanced understanding of local culture and history, and feeling strong emotional connection to the country. Furthermore, the chapter discusses how the advantages once enjoyed by ABC professionals have begun to wane as they find their positions threatened by a wave of talented, highly educated *haigui*.

Chapter 5 focuses on the gendered context of China and how local patriarchal dynamics shape the decision-making and trajectories of female and male ABC professionals. Although both women and men enjoyed comparable career growth and opportunities, their experiences diverged in the social and romantic realms. For single heterosexual men, their foreign citizenship, American educations, and higher wages—in addition to their Chinese ancestry—transformed them into highly eligible dating and marriage partners in the PRC. On the other hand, these same attributes stigmatized their female counterparts, an unexpected reversal of the women's experiences in the United States. Thus, single heterosexual ABC women were forced to prioritize either their professional or their personal lives in China, while their male counterparts could enjoy both. By using an intersectional approach, this chapter reveals the often-overlooked gendered aspects of this form of migration.

The conclusion discusses the larger implications of this study for ancestral homeland migration to the PRC. Furthermore, I explore the negative social effects of the devastating coronavirus pandemic on the lives of ABCs in the United States, as broader cultural acceptance of Asian Americans has plummeted. The return of the harmful stereotype of Asians as a threatening, disease-bearing yellow peril has reinforced the perpetual foreignness of Chinese Americans in their country of birth. The conclusion examines these issues, both on the microlevel of individual experience and on the macrolevel in terms of increasingly fraught U.S.-China relations.

2

Growing Up In-Between

*Chinese American Identity and Belonging
in the United States*

In March 2018, a second-generation Chinese American man named Tony Kao posted a short cell phone video on Facebook. That morning, Kao took a walk with his wife and young son in an upscale, ethnically diverse neighborhood in Southern California. The backdrop of golden sunshine, attractive houses, and regal palm trees provided an unconventional setting for a racist encounter. As Kao's video begins, he tensely addresses a middle-aged white female passing by: "I want you to tell everybody why you told us to go back to our country!" The fiftyish blond woman, dressed neatly in a white cable-knit sweater, fitted blue jeans, and a sun visor, walks away briskly. In a mocking tone, she calls out over her shoulder, "You need to go back to your home country!" Shaking with anger, Kao retorts, "It's unbelievable, at this time and stage, when we're born and raised in the United States, that you told me to go back to my country!" The video cuts off as the woman, stabbing one manicured finger in the air for emphasis, continues to yell that Kao and his family do not belong in America.

The video immediately went viral, garnering nearly seven hundred thousand views within the space of a week. The woman was soon identified as a counselor at a local community college that, ironically, predominantly serves Asian and Latino students. In conversations with the press, she denied that her remarks were racist, saying that they were instead intended to protest the "displacement of European Americans."[1] The public reaction was fierce and immediate, provoking discussions about the growing number of unprovoked racist incidents that had occurred since the start of the Trump administration in 2016.

In an era of smartphones, social media, and the twenty-four-hour news cycle, the American public is inundated with images of racism and racial violence on a scale previously unimaginable. No longer is such abuse known only to its victims. Real-time reporting of police brutality against African Americans, for example, has sparked heightened awareness of the commonplace nature of discrimination faced by people of color. Arguably, part of the reason Kao's video stirred up such an intense reaction—characterized first by shock, then by vitriol—is that popular culture features very few depictions of blatant racism against Asian Americans. In a social context of race that has and continues to be defined by Black–white relations, Asian Americans do not fit neatly into the equation. The Kaos, a young professional couple residing in an upper-middle-class neighborhood, can easily be framed as ideal citizens and embodiments of the American Dream. The reasoning goes, *they* should be safe from unprovoked attacks, insulated by class if not by race. (Note: This has fundamentally changed since the onset of the COVID-19 pandemic in 2020, which I address in the conclusion.)

This video raises complex questions about identity and the limits of belonging for second-generation ABCs today. Slotted into the simplistic dichotomy of model minority or unassimilable foreigner, their rich, nuanced *lived experience* of in-betweenness has historically been underexplored within mainstream culture. Miri Song describes the problematic nature of such ascribed categories: "The wider society's alleged positive perception of Asian Americans has always been ambivalent and rather uneasy—at one moment, Asian Americans may be paragons of the American dream, and at another, they may be ruthless and cunning, as 'Orientals' [who] are seen to be both an economic threat in the Far

East and high achievers who threaten to gobble up places in elite universities."[2]

Stereotypes of Asian Americans that are based on perceived differences from, and proximity to, mainstream white society profoundly affect their construction of identity, particularly when they are growing up. Scholars have noted that some second-generation youths from a variety of ethnic backgrounds use transnational ties to their parental home countries to protect themselves against social exclusion and lack of belonging. This chapter explores these issues for ABCs by examining the impact of transnational ties on their racial and ethnic identities during childhood, adolescence, and early adulthood. In particular, it highlights how the transnational orientations of the second generation vary according to their life stage.[3] Most of my participants felt somewhat excluded from the dominant white culture during childhood and adolescence, which often led to a sense of shame or embarrassment about their ethnic origins, yet in young adulthood, many developed a deep interest in culture, language, and travel in their ethnic homelands, which served as a form of personal empowerment.

Transnational Childhoods

We know a great deal about how first-generation migrants in the United States maintain strong transnational ties, participating in home country activities while simultaneously engaging with their new society. But how does transnationalism shape the identities of their children, who are more directly inculcated into the American hierarchy of race? Second-generation youth grow up between countries and cultures, exposed to their ancestral homelands through family practices and traditions. Even if these young people "rarely visit their ancestral homes or are not fluent in its language," sociologist Peggy Levitt notes, "they are often raised in settings that reference the homeland ideologically, materially and affectively each day."[4]

The people I interviewed were the offspring of post-1965 educational and professional migrants, mostly raised in middle-class white neighborhoods that had good school districts. Their parents' upwardly mobile status, combined with their own educational attainment, allowed these young people to achieve a relatively high level of social integration in their communities. They were also exposed to Chinese cultural traditions that connected them to their ethnic origins in myriad ways, especially through language use and early homeland trips. Still, such parental efforts to maintain culture were generally insufficient in combating their children's feelings of marginalization from mainstream American society.

MAINTAINING LANGUAGE

Immigrant parents commonly use language to retain a sense of community as well as to expose their children to home cultures, yet fluency rates among Chinese American offspring are generally much lower than the rates of their Spanish-speaking counterparts.[5] Among my participants, forty-seven out of sixty were raised in households in which some form of Chinese was spoken. Most learned Mandarin, reflecting the high percentage of those with family roots in Taiwan. Others communicated with their parents in Cantonese, Taiwanese, or more regional dialects, such as Shanghainese. Thirteen respondents used only English at home because their parents spoke different Chinese dialects from one another. The early instillment of these language skills was a key factor cited by ABCs in their later professional success in China.

In a typical example, Robert, a banker I met in Beijing, described himself as a "heritage learner," who could speak Mandarin with ease but lacked more formal grammar skills. "I spoke Chinese growing up. . . . I'm very thankful about that because I would be so lost right now if I hadn't," he expressed. "My reading and writing isn't very good, but I would say that I'm pretty much fluent speaking Chinese, and that's fully attributable to [my parents] speaking Chinese to me growing up. In the house, we would always speak Chinese."

Parents prioritized language to different degrees. Several of my respondents were raised in multilingual Chinese environments. Joanne discussed being taught various dialects that provided her with early insight into the diversity of the Chinese diaspora: "Since my parents grew up in Hong Kong, they mainly spoke Cantonese to each other and so that's what they spoke with me. I also learned to understand Shanghainese through my dad when he spoke to his parents and Wenzhounese when my mom spoke to her parents, so I kind of understood those dialects. We also had a lot of Taiwanese friends, so we spoke Mandarin in the house as well, so it was kind of a random smattering of Chinese dialects all happening."

Another common way that ABC youth developed a transnational orientation was through attending—or, more often, being forced by their parents to attend—weekend Chinese school (known as *zhongwen xuexiao*). First established in the United States in the 1880s, these volunteer-run institutions operate independently from public schools and seek to preserve language and cultural heritage for second- and later-generation ABCs.[6] Going to Chinese school is a commonly accepted (and often widely dreaded) part of Chinese American childhood. Among my sample, half went to Chinese school for at least a short time during elementary or junior high school.

Every Saturday or Sunday morning, *zhongwen xuexiao* classes not only instruct children in basic language but also celebrate Chinese cultural traditions and Confucian values such as filial piety. Perhaps more importantly, they serve as a locus of information sharing and social support for Chinese immigrant parents seeking a supportive community. It was not uncommon for participants' parents to drive an hour or more each way to get their children to these classes. These ethnic educational institutions also play an integral role in helping Chinese immigrant parents adjust to American society and build social networks. "Reconnecting with co-ethnics often helps ease the psychological and social isolation associated with uprooting," writes sociologist Min Zhou. "Co-ethnic ties help connect immigrants to the mainstream society, rather than isolating them from it, by making their social life richer."[7]

Only a handful of the ABCs I spoke with enjoyed Chinese school or believed it was useful, pointing out that once-a-week

Chinese classes taught by volunteers were generally inadequate for perfecting one's language skills. Henry was one of the few with fond memories; reflecting on his six years of Chinese school in New Jersey, he noted that the advantages for his family were more social than educational. "I don't think I learned necessarily all that much Chinese, but it was a great experience," he exclaimed. "You got to meet a lot of people. A lot of exposure to your culture, things like that. It was an avenue for my parents to meet like-minded family and friends as well." At the same time, for Henry, who was born in the PRC, speaking Mandarin at home was the key to maintaining his language skills.

Because most *zhongwen xuexiao* teach Mandarin, they are generally unhelpful for families that speak other dialects, such as Cantonese or Taiwanese. Respondents raised in such households usually attended weekend Chinese school for just a short period of time. Chanson's parents had relocated from Hong Kong to St. Louis, Missouri, when he was a baby. "My parents are Cantonese so I didn't know what was going on," he laughed while recalling his brief experience with Chinese school. "I went to a few classes, and I failed because they kept speaking Mandarin and I couldn't understand what they were saying."

Because most people either felt neutral toward or actively disliked spending their weekend mornings in Chinese school, they attended only as long as their parents insisted. One common avoidance mechanism, which I also employed as a child, was to play a sport that had weekend games. This suggests that for second-generation ABCs, this type of cultural maintenance was neither sufficient nor necessary to affirm their sense of identity and belonging in the United States. Instead, these ethnic institutions were often more important to their immigrant parents, providing venues to exchange child-rearing tips and develop "social capital conducive to [children's] educational achievement."[8]

EARLY HOMELAND TRIPS WITH THE FAMILY

Family vacations to the parental homeland were the second main way individuals engaged in transnational practices during childhood and adolescence. Because the existing research on second-generation homeland trips focuses mainly on adults, these journeys have tended to be understood as forms of ethnic pilgrimage. Thus, it is important to distinguish between homeland trips taken at various stages of the life course and their different underlying motivations. In the case of my respondents, because these early journeys were initiated and planned by their parents, they appeared to have less impact on early identity construction than the future study abroad and homeland travel that many purposefully embarked on as young adults.

In total, forty-one of my participants made at least one return trip with their parents to the PRC, Taiwan, or Hong Kong before high school graduation. Of this group, thirty-one went more than once. However, due to the considerable financial cost and time needed for these journeys, most traveled infrequently. Like Chinese school, ABCs did not consider these trips particularly meaningful, describing them as commonplace childhood events characterized by familial obligation. The words of Richard, age thirty-six, captured a typical sentiment: "I went to Taiwan maybe once every seven years. That's not enough to really have much of an appreciation there, to develop any social ties."

These trips were occasionally motivated by parental desire for cultural-roots seeking—sentiments that did not necessarily transfer down to their children. Ellen, a thirty-two-year-old whose mother was from Hong Kong, described an excursion her family undertook when she was in high school. "It was the first time either of my parents had been back to Asia. My mom had been to Hong Kong once for a high school reunion, but that was the first time my parents had gone to mainland China ever," she explained. "My most poignant memory was my sister and I watching *ER* episodes at the hotel in Guilin. For us, that's like our cool memory. . . . We had a good time, but I really didn't have any of the 'finding my roots' feelings."

Similarly, twenty-seven-year-old Christine went on a family summer trip to Guangzhou to visit her parents' village when she was a teenager. Although it was interesting to meet distant relatives and see her parents' childhood homes, she retained mostly negative memories of the intense heat and challenging living conditions. "I really didn't like it all when I got there. I thought it was really dirty and old," Christine commented. "My aunt that brought us there wanted us to stay for a week, but after two days I was like, 'Get me out of here!' . . . The conditions that they were living in, I was like, 'This is disgusting.'"

Other Chinese immigrant parents took their children back to the ethnic homeland to help preserve the language and culture. George moved from China to the United States at age six and had forgotten all of his Mandarin within two years. As a result, his worried parents sent him back to stay with his grandparents for three months. His family also returned to the Chinese countryside together every two or three years to engage in such traditions as tomb sweeping and praying to ancestors. Even so, as an adult, George did not claim to feel emotionally connected to these early experiences. They had been obligatory, not deeply meaningful.

In her study of second-generation Chinese American young adults in New York City, Vivian Louie argues that parental exposure to the ethnic homeland—through either at-home practices or family return trips—does not necessarily mean that children "will themselves adopt transnational orientations."[9] Early family-driven transnational practices are not particularly effective in creating ethnic pride among second-generation Chinese Americans, likely because the effects are diluted by their more salient experience: being marginalized as racialized minorities in American society.

Ethnic and Racial Ambivalence in Childhood and Adolescence

Perhaps because few of the ABCs I spoke with felt a close emotional connection to their parental homelands while growing up, they tended to experience ambivalent feelings about their ethnic and racial backgrounds during their early lives. Despite the seemingly positive connotations of the model minority label, Chinese Americans are similar to other racialized groups in the United States that use middle-class whiteness as the standard against which they judge themselves. In this way, the youth identities of these ABCs were shaped by internalized racial oppression—the feelings of displacement, embarrassment, shame, or inferiority felt by people of color in the United States due to their racial, ethnic, and cultural differences from the white majority.[10]

Caught between the limiting dichotomy of model minority and perpetual foreigner, the children of Chinese immigrants expend great energy attempting to conform to the structure and expectations of the U.S. racial hierarchy. Rosalind Chou and Joe Feagin argue that Asian Americans often find it necessary to downplay their ethnic and racial backgrounds to find social acceptance, "passively accept[ing] that they must hide or abandon their home cultures, values, and identity to prevent future mistreatment."[11] This constant self-monitoring and judgment can come at a severe psychological cost. Consequently, Asian Americans tend to suffer the effects of racism quietly, causing them to feel "stressed, embattled, isolated, and inadequate" in ways generally overlooked by the rest of society.[12] It is a kind of double invisibility.

EARLY EXPERIENCES OF RACE AND RACISM

My own childhood was largely positive and fulfilling, though looking back, I can see that it was also true that I consistently tried to downplay my Chinese heritage and yearned to be white. I came of age during the 1980s and early 1990s, before the celebration of multiculturalism or nuanced discussions of racial and ethnic identity. Throughout the years, I felt subtle pressure from otherwise well-meaning schools, peers, and the surrounding community to subsume my Asianness in order to assimilate to the norms of my affluent Southern California beach town. One-third of this upper-middle-class suburb consisted of East Asian residents, who had been drawn by the excellent public school system, yet the dominant cultural paradigm was unquestionably that of whiteness.

Early memories of racial and ethnic exclusion have stayed with me, and I can easily bring them to the surface. At age seven or eight, I was walking around my elementary school one afternoon when a white boy named Keith (a known bully) approached menacingly. "Ching Chong, Ching Chong, Ching Chong!" he yelled a foot from my face, pulling his eyelids back severely in hateful mockery. Large and angry, he took clear pleasure in blocking my way as I tried to escape, fearful of a physical attack. Cackling with high-pitched laughter, he finally let me go. Another foundational incident occurred in junior high during a shop class taught by Mr. Boyd, a hypermasculine blond white man in his forties, whose skin was sunburnt the shade of a cherry tomato. The first day of class, I needed to obtain his signature. When my turn came, before I could open my mouth, he looked at me quizzically and enunciated his words in painful slow motion: "Can you speak English?" I stood there, stunned and embarrassed. "Yes, of course I can!" I answered quickly to dispel any of his doubts.

None of these early experiences were particularly unique, painful, or damaging. However, they were integral in shaping my early self-identity: through others' eyes, I saw myself as racially and ethnically different from the norm and, as a result, believed that others might question my Americanness or make me a target of bullying and mockery. From a young age, I knew instinctively that being white was something that could make one's life easier in the United States.

Among my participants, there were certain gendered differences in their recollections of childhood and adolescence, with more women recalling either a desire to be white or a general lack of awareness of racial differences and more men recounting incidents of negative comments and overt racial hostility.[13] Importantly, the small number of ABCs raised by parents who explicitly instilled in them a strong sense of Chinese cultural pride or who grew up in majority Asian immigrant neighborhoods that maintained strong ties to ethnic homelands were more insulated from the negative effects of internalized racial oppression.

For the ABC women I interviewed who grew up in mostly white contexts, whiteness served as an aspirational—albeit unachievable—standard. Julia, a twenty-nine-year-old educational consultant who attended an exclusive private school in the San Francisco Bay Area, described her sense of surprise upon realizing that she was not white when she reached her early teens. "Up until about seventh grade I didn't really identify as Chinese American whatsoever or identify or relate at all to China or Chinese culture," Julia said. "I didn't really identify as Chinese American or ethnically Chinese. I even have a memory of looking in the mirror at about twelve or thirteen and [thinking,] 'Oh, I'm not white?!' Partly because of the schools that I went to, there were few of us who were people of color. The rest were white."

Similarly, Cindy, who grew up in central California, did not identify as ethnically Chinese in her youth, even though her parents were highly integrated into the local Taiwanese American community and founded the local Chinese school. She was not ashamed of her ethnic background, yet whiteness was the unquestioned benchmark against which Cindy defined herself. "We knew we were Chinese because my best friends were always Caucasian and they would come over and be like, 'What is this food that you're eating?'" she recalled. "But I guess I was never really connected to the fact that I was ethnically Chinese. I *was* ethnically Chinese," Cindy clarified, "but I wasn't really a *Chinese person*."

While in Beijing in 2014, I met an academic researcher named Lina, who had grown up outside Boston and attended an overwhelmingly white New England liberal arts college. When I asked whether she had ever experienced racial or ethnic discrimination in her youth, Lina thought for a long time. "I don't think so," she finally answered. "Although in retrospect, I suspect I did but I didn't notice." Lina's early internalization of whiteness had effectively blocked any self-awareness of racism, even that which might have been directed at her. Speaking slowly, she commented about discrimination: "I didn't feel it because I went to school with pretty much all white kids. Chinatown was a place to go eat dinner, but I never really knew any other Chinese kids." Her voice gained more clarity as she began recognizing the role that race may have played when she was young: "My entire life has been like this white prep school. [Classmates] used to call me the whitest girl they've ever met. *I was whiter than the white people.* Maybe that was racist,

I don't know. It just never occurred to me. I just didn't have much Chinese identity really at all."

By comparison, most of the men in this study were unable to deny difference and often felt excluded or at least not fully accepted by their white peers. Many recalled being the targets of racial comments and bullying in grade school. Richard, a thirty-six-year-old who grew up in Texas with Taiwanese immigrant parents, recalled that one white male student made it a point to call him "chink" every day during the ninth grade. Only in hindsight did he realize that being immersed in white American culture was an obstacle to his formation of racial and ethnic identity. "Because my surroundings were so European American, I didn't really have an understanding of what it meant to be Chinese American," he remarked. Looking back, Richard wished that his parents had encouraged him to build a stronger sense of cultural pride: "[My parents] saw that I had no real interest in Chinese culture or Taiwanese culture, so they never really made it a priority to help me understand the importance of understanding that or being proud of it. I think to them, they figured, 'Oh well, Richard will just be American,' and that's that, not realizing the unique identity issues that can arise for the second generation. So the Eurocentric environment that I was brought up in was all I really knew, and I internalized the standards of what is attractive, standards of beauty, and the norms of white culture." Others, such as Brian from North Carolina (whose mother was principal of the local Chinese school), believed that their social marginalization stemmed from not only racial difference but also academic achievement. As Brian said, "I was made to feel different because I was a nerd first and then Asian second. It became more clear in high school for the Asian part, you know. People would be like 'ching chong' and all that. But I was always really combative about it, so I would say negative stuff back to them. My high school was the largest in North Carolina, in terms of student population; it was like three thousand students, but only twenty were Asian or Indian."

Those who did not go by Westernized first names were particularly vulnerable targets for racialized comments. One man who kept his Chinese name after moving to the United States from Taiwan at the age of seven remembered being made fun of constantly. "Caucasian kids are in a way more racist than black kids or other minorities," he commented. The white kids would "see you and do kung-fu noises and stuff." Notably, my participants tended to accept these racist and xenophobic incidents as an inevitable part of American childhood.

PARENTAL LESSONS ON CULTURAL PRIDE

Not everyone I interviewed grew up feeling that Chinese American was an inferior status. Several people described how their parents inculcated a strong sense of ethnic belonging that helped them better navigate the tricky racial terrain of childhood and adolescence. Steve, who had lived in Beijing for nearly two decades, grew up in an all-white part of upstate New York. He marveled at the skill with which his mother and father had raised their children to feel pride and belonging in *both* Chinese and American cultures. "[My parents] encouraged us to feel bicultural. They just never believed that it was an inherent contradiction, and they encouraged us to believe that we were legitimate heirs to great traditions," he recollected. "I think that's one of the many things that my parents did really well that set me on the path that I ended up on. So, they were ferociously proud about their Chinese heritage and . . . they really, really embraced America, American values, everything."

Similarly, Joanne, who grew up in a mostly white suburb in New Jersey, gained a strong sense of cultural pride from her parents, which allowed her to deflect negative racial comments during childhood. She stated, "My parents really tried to instill a sort of pride, a cultural pride, and just made sure that I knew where I came from and appreciated my background. And so [being Chinese] was always something that I identified with. I guess it was a little bit of a challenge not growing up in a predominantly Asian neighborhood, and kids would make fun of me for being Chinese and say stupid things. It bothered me but I just kind of didn't pay attention to that stuff."

Twenty-two-year-old Kimberly also attributed her positive feelings about her Chinese ancestry to her parents. Coincidentally, she and I grew up in the same California suburb, but her family purposefully maintained strong cultural values. Kimberly juxtaposed her pride in being Chinese with her other Asian American friends, who, in her words, "wished they were white." She reflected, "A lot of people of color that grow up in predominantly white neighborhoods experience that 'I wonder what it would be like to grow up in a white family and not have all of these weird family traditions and these weird things over the holidays and whatnot.' But I think growing up, my parents really instilled very traditional Chinese cultural values in my sister and I, and that really stuck with us. So I definitely feel that my Chineseness has really pervaded through my growth." For Kimberly, being continually perceived as "very Chinese" by her Asian American peers eventually became a self-fulfilling prophecy. It would later become the catalyst for her decision to study Mandarin intensively and move to Beijing for work after college.

ETHNIC ENCLAVES AS CENTERS OF IDENTITY AND BELONGING

Beyond having parents who explicitly taught them to value their Chinese heritage, those of my participants who grew up in Asian/Asian American ethnic enclaves that had durable transnational ties back to Asia did not confront the same feelings of ambivalence or internalized racial oppression as those who grew up in majority white areas. The five people who fit this category described their neighborhoods as key sources of ethnic pride that helped them to develop early positive associations with being Chinese American.

Two women I interviewed grew up in Flushing, Queens, in New York City, a major destination for Taiwanese and mainland Chinese migrants since the early 1990s. According to the 2010 census, roughly 70 percent of Flushing's population is Asian, compared to less than 10 percent white.[14] Joy moved from Taiwan to Flushing in elementary school. Now thirty-four, she told me how residing in a Chinese ethnic enclave helped preserve deep connections to her cultural origins: "There's Chinese baths, a Chinese library, Chinese food, Chinese banks. . . . Growing up in Flushing [wasn't] the true American experience given we're so tied back to Asian culture there. You feel like you never really left." She continued, "I feel like I still have a very strong tie to Chinese culture. I don't write that well but I can read perfectly. I can speak Chinese perfectly. I think that's because I was growing up somewhere that I always had a very strong tie back to my roots."

Another woman, a twenty-nine-year-old lawyer named Lili, was born and raised in Flushing. Growing up, she often served as a cultural and language translator—also known as a language broker—between Mandarin and English speakers in her community. "There are a lot of people who live in Flushing who never speak English. I was always very aware of my ethnicity from a young age, and I became very proud of it," Lili proclaimed.

The three other individuals in this group grew up in Asian ethnic enclaves in California. When I asked Howard, who hailed from Cerritos, a city in Los Angeles County with a majority-Asian population,[15] about his experience with ethnic and racial discrimination during childhood, his eyebrows shot up in surprise. "Absolutely not! No. Because everybody was Asian," he exclaimed half-jokingly. "Everybody. Once in a while you saw a white person and maybe you thought they were lost. I'm serious, it was not common."

Fitting in with the ethnic majority in these enclaves provided a sense of comfort that other ABCs could only experience in college or once they moved to the parental homeland. Kelly grew up in a predominantly Asian neighborhood in central California, although her parents primarily used English at home and did not take any family homeland trips. She recalled her envy of classmates whose families maintained strong connections to Taiwan. Unlike the more common scenario of wanting to be white or seeking to hide one's cultural origins, living in a mostly Asian American environment caused her to yearn for *more* exposure to Chinese culture and language: "[My siblings and I] grew up around a lot of Taiwanese immigrants and they all spoke really great Chinese. We were the ones who couldn't speak very much Chinese so I felt like my parents were strange. We never went back to Asia when we were growing up. . . . I would watch my friends go back to Taiwan and bring back cool mechanical pencils and pencil boxes and I'd be so jealous, like, 'Why did they get all the cool stuff?' . . . I felt like I was more Americanized than my classmates. They were cooler because they got to go abroad, and I never got to take a plane anywhere."

These stories all emphasize the importance of social context as well as the malleability of identity and belonging for the second generation, even within the United States.

From Ethnic Ambivalence to Pride in Young Adulthood

Over time, many ABCs undergo major transformations in self-perception. Early negative feelings about their cultural backgrounds can later transform into a sense of self-empowerment. In their study of Asian American adults in the Midwest, Trieu and Lee found that "individuals can (and do) shift out of perceptions and behaviors that perpetuate internalized racism."[16] This can be the result of learning more about ethnic and racial history, getting involved with co-ethnic organizations, and developing more ties with other Asian Americans.

Much of this discovery occurs during college, so often a transition point for personal identity—no matter who you are. According to Nazli Kibria, college often touches off the beginnings of "ethnic collectivity" in which ABCs "self-consciously understand themselves as belonging in an Asian American community."[17] Accordingly, many of my participants recalled their late teens and early twenties as the first time they felt pride in being Chinese American. These identity shifts led to a range of positive outcomes, including more self-acceptance, involvement in Asian American political issues and social causes, and the decision to study or travel in the ancestral homeland.

Most of the people I talked to were aware of their ethnic and racial differences from a young age, but for some this awareness was only sparked in college, when they came into contact with large groups of Asian Americans for the first time. Two women who joined Asian American sororities described discovering a new sense of belonging. Michelle, for instance, grew up in a white suburban neighborhood in Ohio, where she had come to view her American and Chinese identities as totally separate. Not until arriving at the University of Michigan did she comprehend that there was a specifically *Asian American* identity. "That was the first time I saw other Asian Americans and I realized that there was a whole separate culture, a whole separate identity associated with it," Michelle recalled. "And on a certain level I did identify with them more. It was something I'd never really experienced."

Similarly, Cindy had grown up with mostly white friends and identified very little with her ethnicity until she started school at UCLA. "It was interesting to me to be around so many Asians all at once," she stated. "And you felt a difference because it's a bit unspoken and you can't really pinpoint it, but I think the fact that you come from similar backgrounds makes you connect so much easier, and I hadn't had that feeling before." Asked whether joining an Asian American sorority made her feel more connected to Chinese culture, Cindy answered, "I don't think it necessarily made me feel more connected to [the] culture per se." It did, however, increase her self-acceptance of ethnicity. Eventually she married an ABC classmate from college, a decision that initially shocked her family because she had previously only ever dated white men.

Ethnic collectivity also emerged in college as students expanded their knowledge of Asian American history and social issues. For some, learning about the racial exclusion and social marginalization of past and present generations of Asian Americans sparked feelings of anger that led to political engagement. Jonathan, who grew up in a diverse part of Los Angeles, described his undergraduate years as a period of heightened awareness of American race relations:

When you're younger everyone kind of hung out together, it didn't matter what color you were. The white kids hung out with the Chinese kids. In high school the white kids tried to basically hang out with the white kids, the Chinese kids with the Chinese kids, the black kids with the black kids. There was some intermingling . . . but your default is what [race] you are. So I was noticing that more, and then in college—I don't know if it was all the Asian American studies classes I took or not—but you began becoming really angry about it. You're like, "Why the hell is it this way? What's going on?" I do think it goes a little bit far in hindsight, but back then you started looking at all these things that you didn't take as racism. But it's like, "You know, that *is* racist!"

In comparison, Lili credited Asian American studies classes with exposing her to the notion of a pan-Asian social identity, rooted in shared experiences of racial marginalization. Although all her grade school friends in Flushing were of Chinese descent, Lili did not identify as Asian American until college:

I didn't at that point really identify with Asian America because I [considered myself] Chinese. . . . My family didn't come in the 1800s through the railroad. But I did take an Asian American studies class my freshman year in college, and I think that that piqued an interest. I started attending these Asian American political [groups] . . . and so I became really, really involved with all these initiatives. . . . During that time, I realized that even though these things might not be targeting me or Chinese culture or Chinese people in particular—maybe Korean American or whatever—we're all grouped together in this one census box, you know? And so it didn't matter. . . . We're still the minority and people still face discrimination.

Amid their growing consciousness of ethnic identity, racial discrimination, and Asian American social issues, people's college experiences were also influenced by the model minority stereotype. For example, Jenny was heavily involved in student leadership and described a tense race-based dispute that erupted between an Asian American fraternity and the campus Black Student Union. Although Jenny attempted to take a neutral stance, an African American administrator accused her of supporting the fraternity solely due to racial affiliation. She soon dropped out of student government and shifted her focus to international issues. Six years later, Jenny still felt bitter about the situation. "After that incident, I just decided that I didn't want anything to do with domestic politics anymore. It was dirty. It was bad. People will never treat an Asian like a real minority," she exclaimed. "Especially [at my university,] where it was like 50 percent Asian and we were barely a minority on campus. There was always this sense that my voice won't really matter in identity politics in the U.S. because I'll never be taken seriously as a minority."

Alternatively, I spoke with James, whose opinions on race clashed with those of many of his peers when he attended UC Berkeley in the early 2000s. During college, he lived in an Asian American–themed house in which racial discrimination was a constant source of discussion. "We talked about how much we were discriminated against" and how "we were just like the worst-off minority," he said, shaking his head in disbelief as he sat across from me in a Beijing coffee shop. With wry honesty, James described how, in retrospect, being considered a model minority had actually benefited him in his troubled youth. His ability to invoke this stereotype for personal protection led him to believe that Asian Americans could not legitimately claim racial hardship:

> In terms of scale, African Americans have it way worse. It was the source of many arguments for me in college [because] I felt like I was always very lucky, you know. I felt like all the things that Asian Americans complain about are incredibly helpful to me because . . . I didn't fall into the stereotype. Like, I was a very bad kid, and I got into a lot of trouble as a kid, but because people saw me as the Asian American stereotype, I didn't get into worse trouble, either in confrontations with the police or [with] professors who cut me slack or whatever. Like they saw

me, "Oh, he's that Asian kid. He's probably not the one who's at fault here." So I was always given the benefit of the doubt.

James was the only person to speak so pointedly about the potential benefits of being considered a model minority. Some research also concurs. One study of Asian American adolescents states that "being portrayed as a model minority could have some advantages, at least when pitted against the effects of more negative discriminatory views."[18] The authors suggest that not only does the American public view Asian Americans through the lens of high academic achievement, intrinsic ability, and strong work ethic, but also these positive traits are internalized by Asian Americans and can increase their self-confidence. However, they are careful to note that this does not negate the very real harm that this stereotype can create for those who do not fit the criteria.

Connecting to Roots: Study Abroad and Independent Travel in Young Adulthood

The newfound feelings of cultural pride that many individuals experienced during college heightened their curiosity about their Chinese cultural heritage and ancestral roots. As a result, about 40 percent of respondents either chose to study abroad in the PRC as undergraduates or spent extensive periods of time there directly after graduation. Compared to the parent-driven homeland trips they took during childhood or adolescence—which were not that emotionally meaningful—these self-directed journeys were markedly different. They also happened to take place during a pivotal period of growth and change in China.

For many, these independent travels served as the primary catalyst for them to move to the PRC later for professional purposes. For example, Mark, a forty-year-old journalist whose parents were from Guangdong Province, described a summer study abroad experience in Beijing as a defining milestone of his life. "I was absorbing everything I saw with very fresh eyes," he recalled. "I was very excited about China, and I always wanted to come here because of my family background. I knew from then on that I wanted to come back and work here." After taking several other international assignments, Mark moved to Beijing when he was thirty-five.

Elsa, a financier in Beijing, was born in Shanghai and returned there for her junior year study abroad in 1999. Reminiscing fondly, she compared the dynamism of the PRC at that time to the more bureaucratic, staid atmosphere of the United States. "I loved it! Shanghai was raw. It was original," she exclaimed. "Everything in China back then, there were no rules. Whereas in the U.S. there were a lot of rules about everything. In China, it was like the Wild Wild West." When asked why she had felt so free, Elsa referenced the ease that comes with fitting in with the ethnic majority. "It was the freedom about being yourself. Because I am Chinese, I look Chinese. Being here you are a part of the greater masses, so you don't stand out, and you can do whatever you want."

Unlike the rote memorization that defined their childhood Chinese school classes, some used language learning to deepen their ties to the ancestral homeland and create a stronger sense of cultural belonging when they were young adults. After spending a semester in Shanghai during college, twenty-four-year-old Candace decided to work in Beijing directly after graduation. Like Elsa, she relished the freedom of blending in. "I could be walking around and feel invisible. In a good way," she clarified, "not like I wasn't being seen." Candace described how language enhanced the connection she felt to local people during study abroad: "Chinese acquaintances and friends [would] ask me, 'When did you come back?' 'Which province are you from?' 'What's your hometown?' Also, the convention of people referring to other people with familial terminology like 'little sister,' 'big sister,' 'auntie,' this kind of stuff." Sounding nostalgic, she discussed her heightened feelings of cultural belonging at that time: "I felt like the language was inviting me to treat China as a homeland, and I think, being a student of language at that time, I was like, 'This is it!' This is what I was reaching for. . . . I could feel a sense of belonging both in America and [in] China."

Study abroad thus became an opportunity to reconcile thorny issues of personal identity in the United States. Jonathan spent his junior year in Beijing during the late 1990s. Now in his mid-thirties, he laughed aloud when describing the personal angst that motivated his journey to China. "I just really had a deep desire to go back to China, like the 'motherland China,' and see what life was like there," he explained. Through his travels, Jonathan's involvement with the ancestral homeland helped him cope with feelings of racial marginalization in the United States.[19]

During study abroad, Jonathan engaged in a roots-seeking trip to the Chinese countryside, where he visited his father's birthplace and met distant relatives. This quasi family reunion provided a visceral sense of blood-based belonging that helped his younger self resolve pressing identity-based issues. In that pre-smartphone era, Jonathan's father provided haphazard instructions for locating his cousin: "I've never met him, you've never met him, so I'll just have him write your name on the board and hopefully you can find each other!" However, any concerns of getting lost were assuaged when Jonathan arrived in his father's hometown:

> When I got to the train station—and it was just one of those really run-down ones in the middle of nowhere twenty years ago—I got off and I was looking around the crowd and I saw my name at the same time as I saw this guy's face. And the crazy thing was, I knew it was him. Obviously, my name was on there, but he looked like someone from my family. And it was kind of shocking, but it was also in a way deeply satisfying to see someone that I was truly related to, like phenotypically you could tell this was my family. It was cool, [and] it helped me feel connected in a way. And then I visited his family and they took me to where my dad had grown up and stuff, so I did that whole cultural roots and identity thing, which . . . helped answer some questions. It did help inform whatever gap I was experiencing in that identity stuff.

Jonathan's experience resembles those of other ABCs. For example, Andrea Louie's research on later-generation Chinese

Americans who visited their ancestral villages in Guangdong Province found that these trips deepened their cultural connections to China while helping to clarify their racial and ethnic identities back in the United States. Their roots-seeking experiences allowed these individuals to first "create narratives of family history and personal identity exploration, and then use these narratives to contextualize their lives within the broader picture of Chinese–Asian American experiences."[20] For my respondents, the self-initiated journeys they took as young adults often inspired a long-lasting interest in the ancestral homeland that drew them back again when they got older.

Conclusion

These stories of second-generation Chinese American professionals who later moved to the PRC show how personal identity formation is a fluid and contextual process inflected by the U.S. racial hierarchy, cultural stereotypes about Asian Americans, and transnational ties to parental home countries. During childhood and adolescence, most participants either aspired to be white or felt as if they needed to downplay or hide their ethnic heritage. In young adulthood, many found a sense of belonging through learning more about Chinese history, language, and culture, as well as through homeland travel.

Some scholars contend that growing up in households that maintain transnational ties is highly useful for American-born children of immigrants. Peggy Levitt, for example, has argued that being socialized into two different cultural and national settings benefits second-generation youth by allowing them to "master several cultural repertoires that they can selectively deploy in response to the opportunities and challenges they face."[21] I have found, however, that parental maintenance of culture through Chinese language school and early family return trips did not necessarily help children combat feelings of social inferiority and marginalization. In other words, these types of transnational practices were typically no match for the pernicious effects of internalized racial oppression experienced by Chinese American children and adolescents growing up in mostly white communities.

Nevertheless, college represented a time of burgeoning ethnic pride and expanded understandings of these young people's racial and cultural identities, often leading to involvement with Asian American political issues and self-initiated homeland travel. Through finding ethnic collectivity, the ABCs I spoke with came to view being Asian American as not just "an identity imposed from the outside but a notion to be actively embraced."[22] By pure happenstance, personal identities that shifted from ethnic ambivalence to belonging happened to coincide with the formative years of China's global economic rise. These individuals were thus uniquely positioned to capitalize on their biculturality, their language skills, and the cultural connection gained from earlier homeland trips when they later relocated to their ethnic homeland to build their careers.

3

Creating the "Non-American American Dream" Overseas

Strategic In-Betweenness in Action

A *Wall Street Journal* article from 2011, titled "U.S.-Born Chinese, Back in China to Set Up Shop," highlighted the trend of Chinese Americans "returning" to their ancestral homeland to build careers. The article featured Austin Hu, a Wisconsin-born chef who, at only thirty-one years old, had already opened and was managing his own Western fine-dining restaurant in Shanghai (where he opened another successful restaurant in 2017). Acknowledging the tremendous financial opportunities that he encountered in the PRC, Mr. Hu commented, "I'm Chinese-American, but I'm not a mainlander. I respect the energy here, though. This is a place where you can make something of yourself regardless of where you came from. It's the non-American American dream."[1]

The article's title implied that Mr. Hu had returned to a place of inherent cultural belonging. Despite his co-ethnic background, however, the distinction he drew between himself and mainlanders suggests that, at least from his perspective, he exists somewhere *between* foreign and local. This chapter explores this ethnic and cultural in-betweenness for second-generation ABCs in China. As detailed in the introduction, in-betweenness can create feelings of social marginalization for young Chinese Americans in the

United States. However, upon moving to the ancestral homeland—one in which key economic sectors are still developing—in-betweenness becomes a tool that these highly educated first-world migrants can use to create personal career advantage.

Chinese Americans often do not feel acknowledged as "real Americans" in either the United States or the PRC. Their physical features, their ethnic backgrounds, and the biologically based notions of cultural belonging pervasive in both societies cause others to presume that they are somehow innately Chinese. Though limiting, these simplistic assumptions of ethnic, racial, and cultural belonging allowed the ABCs I met in Beijing and Shanghai to become indispensable bridges between Western and Chinese business interests during a key era of economic development. In conjunction with the Chinese government's desire to cultivate "high quality" skilled workers to help raise the nation's global status, these individuals found themselves to be well positioned for financial opportunity.[2]

My respondents both strategically and consciously capitalized on their in-betweenness in the ancestral homeland, leveraging their American skills and training and their assumed knowledge of Chinese culture for personal gain. Their success hinged on the ability to deftly maneuver between different categories of cultural, ethnic, and national belonging by consciously altering how they presented themselves to others. At the same time, they often evoked Americanness in the workplace in ways that created social distance between themselves and local people.

For Money More Than Love: Motivations for Moving to China

Chapter 2 discussed how many of the Chinese Americans I interviewed had engaged with the country earlier in their lives through study abroad programs and independent travel, motivated by the desire for cultural connection. Young adulthood (roughly up to age twenty-five) was, for my respondents, a key period of ethnic discovery, often characterized by intensified curiosity about Chinese society and grappling with identity-based issues. Most of those who traveled to the PRC returned to the United States to obtain more training, typically earning higher degrees or gaining several years of work experience in American companies before relocating to Beijing or Shanghai.

At the time of our interviews, most individuals were between the ages of twenty-five and thirty-five. Compared to younger ABCs, people in this age range appeared less interested in connecting with culture or exploring identity-based issues. For example, thirty-two-year-old Ellen was the daughter of a Taiwanese father and Hong Kongese mother. Despite having resided in Beijing for six years and being married to a Chinese native she met there, the entrepreneur emphasized her lack of a strong cultural tie to the PRC. "I don't feel this roots/homeland thing," Ellen explained. "I haven't been to either of the towns my parents' families are from because to me, it means nothing." She believed it would be more personally meaningful to trace her parents' migration trajectories and early experiences in Boston and New York Chinatowns rather than in a homeland they had left behind decades earlier.

Along similar lines, I spoke with Stephanie, a thirty-nine-year-old writer who reluctantly moved to Shanghai three years earlier when her husband was offered a highly coveted position. Speaking loudly over the chatter of other customers at a popular restaurant, she compared her approach to roots seeking to her own parents' intense curiosity. "I can't say that I'm that interested in where my *laojia* [native village] is. Like, my parents would visit every May. They're in Hunan [Province] right now, checking out where my grandfather grew up. I'm not that interested in it, to be honest. For me [China's] more a place with career opportunities," she stated. "Everyone was like, 'Oh you're going to come here and research your family roots and write a book.' I was like, 'Well, it's not really what interests me.'"

This ambivalence toward ancestral roots can be contrasted with that of second-generation Indian American professionals in India, who resemble ABCs in terms of parental migration trajectories to the United States, class status, skills, and educational attainment. In her research, sociologist Sonali Jain finds that her Indian American respondents tend to profess strong affective ties to their ancestral homeland, often "constructing both the U.S. and India as 'home.'"[3] Perhaps a key difference is that nearly all of Jain's respondents had multiple relatives living in India, whom they visited for extended periods of time during childhood. By contrast, most of my respondents' families were divided by the Chinese Communist Revolution, which drastically cut off contact between those who fled to Taiwan and those who remained behind from the late 1940s to the late 1970s. Thus, while many of the ABCs I interviewed took summer family trips to Taiwan or China when they were young, they did not visit with the same regularity and typically stayed for shorter periods than did their Indian American counterparts, who usually stayed for entire summers.

For numerous individuals, Taiwan symbolized more of an emotional homeland than the PRC. I spoke with a corporate executive named Joy who spent part of her childhood in Taiwan. "I had never really been to China growing up, so no, it's not much of a return because my homeland is Taiwan," she reasoned. "If you want to 'return,' you have to [first] recognize it as a home-land." Others struggled with ambivalence toward expectations of emotional connection with their parental homeland. In Beijing, I chatted for several hours with Maria, a thirty-nine-year-old international development worker who had moved there a year earlier and still seemed somewhat perplexed by her decision. Professing more of an affinity with central Asian cultures, Maria grappled with her lack of emotional resonance with China based on shared ethnic ancestry: "I'd always felt very ambivalent about China being my emotional homeland, even though I'm of Chinese heritage. I've met people here who are not of Chinese heritage at all but who have such a clear emotional connection to China. It's what enables them to learn the language so quickly, and to understand the customs, and to feel so at ease with the people. I don't feel that about China. I never have. That is probably the biggest surprise because oftentimes we're expected to have an identity that lines up really nicely with how we look."

Not even those who were born in the PRC tended to view the country as an emotional homeland. Kevin, a filmmaker in his late twenties, was born and raised in Shanxi Province until age nine, when his parents moved the family to Los Angeles. Because they did not make any return trips when he was young, his parents' memories of Chinese society predated the sweeping transformations brought about by economic reforms and modernization efforts. Peggy Levitt has called this the "ossification effect," in which "migrants cling to . . . their memories" while "their homelands have moved on."[4] When Kevin moved to Beijing, his local co-workers teased him for using outdated words and speaking style. Three years later, having become accustomed to local language and customs, Kevin described his parents as "a time capsule" of Chinese people in the 1990s. In returning to his birth country as a young man, Kevin found that his romanticized notions of homeland were wildly inaccurate. "My memory of what China was or what I thought was my homeland is totally not there," he reflected. "I think I left China at such a young age, I didn't really develop this feeling of affinity to the country." Kevin's need to reconcile a remembered homeland with the reality of the country today highlights "the fluidity of 'homeland' as both a theoretical and material construct, where a sense of national affiliation or belonging can be as much imagined as it is remembered."[5]

Emotional longing, therefore, tended to be outweighed by financial and professional motivations for moving to China. When I asked Christine, a twenty-seven-year-old public relations executive, about her decision to move to Beijing five years earlier, she exclaimed, "All of it is economic! Especially if you're talking about ABCs—the ones . . . born in America [who] don't really have family here—it's all economic." Even for those who traveled and studied abroad in China as young adults, by the time they reached their mid- to late twenties, cultural reasons were less important factors than economics in the decision to relocate. This group included Benjamin, who studied abroad in Shanghai in college, worked for a decade as a financial consultant in the United States, and then moved back to Shanghai with his Taiwanese American wife in their early thirties to start their own businesses. He was candid about this second move: "Coming here, the decision was like 80 [percent economic], 20 [percent cultural]. Even like 90/10. I came here to make money, to be honest."

These sentiments emerged repeatedly throughout my conversations. I met with George, a twenty-six-year-old Harvard graduate who left China at age six and moved to Shanghai after college to work as an investment adviser. Seated across from me in a dim, noisy expat bar, the soft-spoken young man described his motivations for returning. "It's definitely not connection to roots," he stated matter-of-factly. Adjusting his fashionable metal-rimmed glasses, George elaborated, "[I came here for] economic opportunity, and the fact that my competitive advantage is in China. If I go back to the States now, I would be disadvantaged compared to my peers. I wouldn't have the experience in the top tier investment banks that they might have. I wouldn't have the network that they have. But because I've been in China these four years, I speak Chinese. I know the lay of the land."

Employing shrewd market logic, many respondents coupled learning more about Chinese culture with furthering their financial goals. Steven, a twenty-five-year-old banker who left the PRC as a toddler, described his choice to return as being driven by "80 percent economic reasons, 20 percent getting back in touch with my roots." He explained how being knowledgeable about the dual realms of economics and culture could benefit him personally: "Given China's economic prowess in the world, on the world stage, I think those two [spheres] are slowly becoming one and the same. Getting back in touch with my roots can serve an economic purpose, and coming here for business purposes helps me learn more about Chinese culture as well."

In line with the notion of "strategic switching," in which people migrate at different ages for different reasons, I suggest that my respondents' primarily professional motivations for moving to the ancestral homeland reflected the intensely career-oriented nature of their particular life stage. Jonathan, a thirty-five-year-old corporate attorney who later became a partner in his firm, viewed his current position through the lens of professional achievement; this was a major shift from the yearning for cultural connection that drove him to study abroad in Beijing in college, as detailed in chapter 2. Jonathan's identity, too, had shifted dramatically over time. Now married with children, he looked back on the college years as a time in which people are "so concerned with identity and figuring out who you are, and I think it's important to ask those questions. But then, after a while, you've either figured it out or you've moved on." Gazing out of the floor-to-ceiling window of his high-rise office building and onto the sprawling metropolis below, Jonathan continued: "At some point in life when you become older, your identity is really rooted in your family. Like for me now, where I belong is wherever my family is, and so that's where I put the root of my identity."

Because most respondents felt they had largely resolved pressing issues of ethnic identity and belonging earlier in their lives, only one person I spoke with claimed to have moved to the PRC for purely cultural reasons. Howard, a youthful-looking thirty-eight-year-old psychologist, had relocated to Beijing with his wife and young son to take a job at a Western medical clinic. He sought to improve the country's burgeoning mental health system and, by doing so, contribute to the development of Chinese society. Like many other ABCs in this study, both of Howard's parents were born in China and raised in Taiwan, moved to the United States for education, and later raised their children in a middle-class area with a renowned school district. When we first spoke in 2014, only one year after he had arrived in Beijing, Howard was somewhat dismayed by the common response of Chinese locals after they learned about his background. He explained, "A lot of the people here are like, 'Why did you come back? (a) when your parents worked so hard to leave, and (b) when everybody here is going that way?' [toward the United States]. They're like, 'You speak English. You were educated in the States. You were born in the States. You have the passport. Why would you want to come back here?'"

Howard's decision to uproot his family—taking a major pay cut in the process—arose from a deeply held sense of responsibility and the desire to give back to China in exchange for the many great life opportunities he had received. Seated behind a large desk in his pristine white office, he declared emotionally, "I'm so indebted and grateful to my parents for giving me what they gave me. Not a day goes by where I don't realize and remember that I've been given [a life] that not everybody has." Howard believed that training local people in Western psychological knowledge and practices could "help equalize things a little bit" within Chinese society. Perhaps due to his high expectations of cultural belonging—notably, he had not studied abroad when he was younger—Howard seemed to feel the most out of place in his ancestral homeland. Rather than using in-betweenness to his advantage, he was disappointed by it, noting that mainlanders could immediately sense that he wasn't local from his speaking style, body language, and clothing.

"In the States, I think what shines is my 'Chineseness,' because our skin color is different from the majority and our culture is different from the majority, but here what shines is my 'American-ness,'" he lamented. "I've never felt so American in my life. . . . That's something I wasn't prepared for. I was prepared for this 'I'm coming home' feeling, where I'm coming [back] to the land of my ancestors." Howard's genuine dismay at not feeling fully accepted in China aligns with the experiences of later-generation Asian Americans who embark on temporary homeland tours. During roots visits, "the desire to belong in one's ancestral land leads people to conflate nostalgic imagination with reality," which reinforces the sense of being a cultural outsider in one's homeland.[6]

Of course, these feelings may shift over time as people acclimate to living in China. Four years later I spoke with Howard again and asked him whether he still felt a sense of cultural dislocation. "Yes and no," he answered thoughtfully. "No, in that I still feel very American, but I think I understand a lot more of the Chinese mindset." Howard's extended time in China—which was marked by the birth of a second child and relocation to Shanghai for a new position—allowed him to embrace his cultural in-betweenness rather than be bothered so much by it.

"Who do I identify myself with more? It might be a little bit of a question mark," he pondered. "Whereas before—when we last talked—it was like, 'Oh, yeah, I am totally American.' Right now, you know, not so much. Now I think I've bonded a lot more with Chinese society." Ultimately, Howard viewed his cultural identity as a work in progress. He had become more emotionally attached to the PRC over time. "I don't consider myself Chinese. I'm still an American, culturally [and] in the way that I think," he told me. "But in terms of emotional bonding, I do think I'm a little bit more Chinese. I don't know if I'm mostly Chinese, but I'm a little bit more than I was before."

Moving to China to Bypass the "Bamboo Ceiling"

ABC professionals were able to ascend quickly into management and leadership positions in their Chinese workplaces. In the process, they were able to escape the effects of the so-called bamboo ceiling that hinders Asian Americans from reaching leadership positions in the U.S. corporate world.[7] Studies have found that the underrepresentation of Asian Americans in management prevails, despite educational attainment and average income levels that exceed those of whites. One report that examined 2007–2015 aggregate data from large companies in the San Francisco Bay Area found that "Asians are the least likely to be promoted to managerial or executive positions, in spite of being the largest minority group of professionals and the most likely to be hired."[8] The effects of the bamboo ceiling are especially gendered, with Asian women being the least represented in executive roles. Denise Peck, former vice president at Cisco and coauthor of the report, sharply noted, "Minority women continue to bump against a double-paned glass ceiling."[9] By contrast, white workers, regardless of gender, become executives at twice the rate of Asians.

A *Harvard Business Review* article suggests that the bamboo ceiling has been perpetuated by two negative stereotypes about Asians and Asian Americans in the United States: first, that they are highly competent and therefore threatening to white co-workers, and second, that they do not possess sufficient social skills and are thus unfit for leadership. Consequently, although Asian Americans may be considered "dedicated and intelligent," they are also viewed as lacking "attributes of masculinity, charisma, and tyranny" that are typically associated with executive officers.[10]

Less robust social networks also hinder Asian American corporate leadership. In a study of second-generation Asian American professionals, sociologist Margaret Chin found that although getting a job was not problematic for them, climbing up the ladder proved especially difficult. Many learned that the strategies they relied on to achieve educational success—such as "working hard, being smart, being the best at what you do, and not rocking the boat—were practically useless past the first few junior-level positions in the corporate world."[11] Social factors thus shape racialized perceptions of Asian Americans' competence and leadership abilities in the United States.

In the ancestral homeland, however, these stereotypes do not exist for Chinese American professionals. The uniqueness of their Western educations, English language fluency, and bicultural knowledge facilitate their entrance into key management and leadership roles. As one participant stated, "If you're an ABC in China, you're generally at some level where you're either the expert or somebody higher up, you know. You're not the person starting out." Many individuals experienced vastly accelerated promotions, especially when compared to their peers back home, and were thrust into roles as middle managers soon after arrival. Eric, a successful twenty-eight-year-old architect and restaurateur in Beijing, described how ABCs could use strategic in-betweenness to become trusted and needed advisers—a stance that could quickly enhance their careers. "If you look at an international company [in China], your boss is usually foreign or Hong Kongese, Singaporean, British, or American," he stated. "They obviously aren't as culturally familiar with China as you are, so they always ask you your opinions. You take on that adviser role, which is good, whereas in the States, you're always going to be an intern."

Benjamin, who spent ten years working for companies in the United States that employed numerous highly qualified ABCs, believed that his background helped him to stand out in China. He remarked heartily, "Here, as an Asian American man, there is no ceiling. Anything is possible!" Respondents recognized that being situated somewhere between Western and Chinese cultures allowed them to serve as cultural liaisons in the PRC. For example, Steven noted that compared to other non-Chinese expats, ABCs have a great competitive advantage through their "firm understanding of the language and a firm understanding of the culture of both worlds." He continued, "We are able to bridge that. It's a very interesting place to be."

Among those who possessed the skills needed in quickly developing sectors of China's knowledge economy, age was not a hindrance. Many relatively young people I met were given extensive professional responsibilities. The financial rewards could be great, as twenty-eight-year-old Eric boasted, "My pay level right now is how much I would get paid in the States in twenty years." Likewise, twenty-seven-year-old Christine described the PRC as "a land of opportunity." Her parents had convinced her to return home to Boston after five years abroad. However, Christine bemoaned the unique professional opportunities and access to important people she would forfeit by leaving: "Anything that you want to happen, it can happen [here], especially with work. I'm sad to leave China because being here I've had so much exposure to C-level staff from the U.S. Because I'm the liaison for China, I work directly with global directors in the U.S. or CEOs of Fortune 500 companies. How often can somebody that's in their twenties sit in a room with these CEOs of Fortune 500 companies? It's only because I'm based in China that I get to do this."

Moving to the PRC brought particularly rapid advancement to those who had already obtained substantial work experience in the United States. Alan, a thirty-five-year-old corporate sales manager whom I first interviewed in 2013, skyrocketed up the ranks of his high-tech equipment company after relocating to Shanghai three years earlier. He had worked at a U.S. company for a decade, married, and settled in San Diego before being aggressively recruited to head up the firm's Asia office in 2010. Alan described his meteoric rise upon arriving in China: "I went from technical sales, past the regional manager, past the United States country manager, to controlling one-third of our company's revenue. . . . So I jumped about three or four levels, into now. From a sales standpoint, maybe I was doing US$2 million dollars in sales, US$3 million on a good year, and now I come out here and we're doing about US$40 million. Now I have sales managers, I have country managers, and they have sales managers, then they have salespeople. So it's a really big opportunity for me. If I went back to the United States, I probably wouldn't have this opportunity."

Alan's professional success in China progressed exponentially. When we spoke again in 2018, he had joined a firm that was sold to an American-owned Fortune 500 company. Now serving as the manager of the entire Asia region, Alan was working on setting up branch offices in the United States and Europe. "[These] next couple of years, I'm going to really focus on growing this business for Asia," he said excitedly. "I mean, it's exploded for us! This industry, nothing's happened like this. When I joined this business unit, I had about $100 million of worldwide sales, and within two and a half years, we're at $400 million."

Notably, ABCs' workplace advantages in China did not appear to be gender specific. Men and women alike progressed quickly on the basis of their professional expertise as well as their American citizenship. Many women felt similarly to Lili, a twenty-nine-year-old corporate attorney who told me, "China gives me this feeling of being able to do anything!" Sociologist Kathrin Zippel has termed this phenomenon the ".edu bonus," in which authority and respect is conferred onto Western-educated female professionals who work abroad, thus overcoming localized forms of gender discrimination.[12]

The professional trajectory of thirty-three-year-old Kelly, an entertainment executive, is exemplary of my female respondents. After earning a prestigious U.S. law degree and working in the

Hollywood entertainment industry for several years, she arrived in Beijing to join a foreign-owned media production company. When we met, Kelly had worked demanding hours seven days a week without a break for three months straight. Three years into her time in Beijing, she was successfully juggling the weighty responsibilities of locating projects, negotiating contracts, and putting films into production. It had taken her only six months to be promoted to vice president of operations.

We met on a rare blue-sky day in Beijing in a gleaming new high-rise building in the ritzy Sanlitun district. Ignoring a steady stream of text messages that appeared in rapid succession on her phone, Kelly knew her chances of becoming a high-level manager in the United States were extremely low. "I wouldn't be a VP of anything in the entertainment industry," she commented brightly, "at least not like half a year after I came to the company!" Kelly felt that a specialized combination of factors made her uniquely desirable in China, including the "shortage of people here who have the work experience, who are knowledgeable about the industry, who work hard, and are bilingual."

Hence, educated ABCs were able to capitalize on their cultural capital and professional skills to swiftly climb the ranks within their chosen fields. At the same time, some noted that China's constantly changing, unpredictable environment required tenacity. Jonathan articulated the culture of high risk and reward in working there: "It's exciting! There are a lot more opportunities. It doesn't work for everyone [though] because for the most part training here is like trial by fire, so you really have to learn how to roll with it because people just throw you in . . . because there's no one here to train you, or . . . no one's ever done it before so you're just gonna have to figure it out. So it's really challenging in that way and it doesn't really suit all personality types. And it can be really stressful, but the reward is that we do really interesting stuff and if you do it well, you can rapidly advance. Whereas you don't have those opportunities in the States as much."

The dynamism of their workplaces matched the fast pace of life in China's global cities, providing a sense of unlimited freedom and possibility that many perceived to be lacking in America's highly mature economy. For example, thirty-two-year-old Philip, a corporate salesperson in Shanghai, reveled in having taken a less conventional professional path. He envisioned his likely career trajectory had he stayed in the United States in the following way: "If I was in the States, either in New York or in California, I could probably see what my life would be like in twenty years. I would be in a big corporation, probably a VP, making anywhere from $200,000 to $300,000 a year, house in the suburbs, two cars. I can see how my life would play out. It's pretty predictable."

Although he appreciated the comfort of the American lifestyle, Philip saw limits to what he could achieve professionally in the United States. "Going to China is just more of 'I don't know where it's going to end up, but I know that there are more possibilities,'" he explained. Individuals like him who possessed a more entrepreneurial spirit preferred to take the risk of moving to China to broaden their global perspectives in the hopes of achieving an even better financial outcome.

Profiting from Flexible Ethnicity in the PRC

My conversations made clear that the in-betweenness that can exclude ABCs from full social membership in the United States is reconfigured as a professional advantage for them in China. Their experiences support a social constructionist view of ethnic identity as a dynamic process continually shaped through interaction, rather than a fixed set of shared characteristics. From this perspective, ethnicity is produced through dialectical relationships between ethnic groups and the larger social context or, as Miri Song has written, "between assignment, which is imposed by others in the wider society, and assertion, which is a claim to ethnicity made by groups themselves."[13]

Scholars have argued that ethnicity tends to be optional for white Americans, who can claim ethnic heritage when it interests them but otherwise not incorporate it in a sustained manner.[14] Others suggest that Asian Americans in the United States also enjoy some amount of ethnic flexibility. Unlike African Americans, whose ties to ethnicity were destroyed through the forced migration of slavery, Asian Americans—particularly the highly educated middle class—may choose to actively take pride in their ethnic ancestry.[15] Similar to whites, then, Asian Americans have the freedom to practice "symbolic ethnicity" by celebrating more superficial aspects of their cultural heritage, such as holidays, while choosing not to partake in others, such as learning an ancestral language.[16] Yet as Mia Tuan notes, such ethnic flexibility may be largely limited to the decisions they make in their personal lives.[17]

To varying extents, members of racialized ethnic groups may choose to highlight or mask different features of their identity, depending on the situation and localized understandings of race and ethnicity. Here I employ Jessica Vasquez's concept of "flexible ethnicity," which refers to "the ability to deftly and effectively navigate different racial terrains and be considered an 'insider' in more than one racial or ethnic group."[18] Flexible ethnicity points to the existence of multiple ethnic options, categories that vary according to national context. The ABCs I interviewed could access a much wider range of ethnic options in the ancestral homeland than in the United States, a fact they consciously used to their advantage. As they shifted between different categories through carefully crafted performances, flexible ethnicity became a key aspect of strategic in-betweenness that they wielded to maximize personal gain.

More precisely, my respondents deliberately switched between ethnic, national, and cultural categories depending on the audience and desired outcome. For example, PR executive Christine leveraged locals' assumptions about her cultural expertise to further her own objectives. To impress one important prospective mainland Chinese client, she and her white American boss made the tactical decision that, during meetings, Christine would communicate only in English, while he would use only Mandarin. She described how these scripted presentations elicited positive outcomes for their firm: "[My boss is] a forty-something-year-old Caucasian man that speaks fluent Chinese. I'm a twenty-something-year-old ABC that speaks fluent English. . . . It just felt like a show that we were putting on, like, 'Oh, look at this Chinese girl speak English! Look at this Caucasian guy speak Chinese!' . . . In the eyes of some of our clients, they thought, 'Oh, this is fantastic. I want this international agency. I want these people to build my brand because they understand West, they understand East. It's perfect.'"

As we chatted over coffee in a Starbucks in Shanghai, Christine further divulged how she used flexible ethnicity as a tool to win over clients. "In work settings, people sometimes will think, 'Oh, you're ABC, you understand Western culture completely, so I want to hear your insights on it. But at the same time, you're Chinese so you understand what it is that Chinese people need or want,'" she explained. "In that sense, I feel like they would see the Western side of me or the Chinese side of me and see the benefits of it, *depending on which card I want to play more.*"

ABCs did not just capitalize on their in-betweenness with regard to Chinese mainlanders; they also benefited from incorrect assumptions that white Western peers made about their ethnic identities and cultural knowledge. Financial adviser George found it humorous that non-Chinese expats often projected far more cultural expertise onto him than he actually had. "I think it's funny, because Westerners think you're somehow really [native] Chinese when you're Chinese-American," he explained. "You can sort of play that off, like 'You don't understand—I've been here for four years, I understand how it works,' even if you don't really know how it works. Westerners are like, 'You look Chinese, you *must* know how it works. You must speak perfect Chinese.'"

Others improvised novel strategies. For instance, Philip, a salesperson for a Western-owned company in Shanghai, claimed to be a clueless foreigner while also showing off his cultural knowledge and expertise to gain the trust of both expatriate and local colleagues. Successfully using this tactic required a high level of biculturality and language skills. Fluent in Mandarin and English, Philip was able to switch between groups easily. However, he chose to identify himself as American to local clients. By playing the role of a hapless outsider, he lowered their expectations while simultaneously benefiting from the greater trust granted to those with Chinese heritage. He described how he employed this strategy with Chinese natives: "I always say, 'Oh, you know, I'm American. I don't really know about China' [and] I tend to make myself sound like the stupid foreigner who doesn't know anything. But because I do it in Mandarin and the way I express myself, I blend in with Chinese people quite easily. So I think that it gives me an advantage in a sense that they don't feel a cultural emotional distance from me but at the same time they still think I'm more international."

Philip's approach allowed him to position himself as a liaison between Western upper management and mainland colleagues, giving him insider status with both groups. "You can tell there's a certain gap between them," he explained, "and so for me I think it's good because the Chinese still feel like I'm one of them." By accepting and thus trusting him, the locals were more honest in sharing their opinions and frustrations. At the same time, Philip leveraged his American background to gain the ear of his expat bosses by telling them, "I'm one of you guys. Let me help you understand China!"

Invoking Americanness in Chinese Workplaces

On a hot summer day in June 2013, I met with Paul at the Bookworm, a now-closed coffee shop that was popular with Western expatriates in Beijing. Dressed casually in a T-shirt and jeans, the forty-year-old successful bar and restaurant owner looked much younger than his age. By that point, Paul had lived in China for nearly a decade and had worked in a wide range of fields—including performing arts, journalism, and food and beverage—despite lacking previous experience with any of them. Five years earlier, he became an entrepreneur after realizing that he wanted to be his own boss. After spending a year developing a business concept, recruiting investors, learning restaurant management, and training local staff, he opened a trendy downtown Beijing bar to great acclaim. Two other fashionable high-end bars soon followed. Reflecting on his unlikely and unconventional trajectory, Paul chuckled, "I wouldn't have been able to do this in the States, that's for sure!"

Throughout our conversation, the entrepreneur complained repeatedly about the problem of *chabuduo* (meaning "good enough" or "close enough"), which refers to the cutting of corners and mediocre job performance. Over the years, Paul had become deeply cynical to the point where he equated Chinese work culture with complacency, inefficiency, and getting by with the least possible effort. He waged a constant battle to change this mentality among his local staff. "I never say *chabuduo* and I never accept *chabuduo*!" he exclaimed hotly. "I say, 'You do it exactly or you don't do it. *Chabuduo* is not good enough. Start over!'"

Paul believed that his workers' lax attitudes were a by-product of Chinese cultural norms in which work is dependent on *guanxi* (social connections) rather than individual ability. "It's about who you know," he complained. "It's not about how well you do something. It's about who you're doing it with." Sipping an iced coffee, he compared work in China versus the United States, opining that the individualism inherent in American culture creates more self-motivation and therefore better results: "Most [Chinese] people aren't really proud of their jobs. They're not there to work. They're there for the money. . . . I think it's the *chabuduo* mentality. They grow up with it. 'The government will take care of us.' . . . I don't think there is a culture of, you know, pull yourself from your bootstraps. That's just typically American. And so, this is why my employees all know that I'm American. Because I'm crazy. They think that because I push them. Americans are the only people who do that. Everybody else is almost *chabuduo*. The French are *chabuduo*. The Italians are *chabuduo*. The Spanish are totally *chabuduo*."

ABCs like Paul benefited from their flexible ethnicity in China. At the same time, many evoked Americanness in their workplaces, espousing an idealistic view of work as an individualized calling and source of self-fulfillment that requires people to always do their best. By defining certain qualities such as professionalism, critical thinking skills, and a strong work ethic as uniquely

American traits, they positioned themselves as Western experts whose talents were sorely needed in China. By contrast, they often labeled the Chinese work style as *chabuduo* and considered their greatest contribution to be instilling principles of hard work and high quality into local culture.

Most mainlanders, in their view, lacked commitment to their jobs and produced inconsistent results. Ellen—a friendly, outspoken thirty-two-year-old social entrepreneur from Southern California—ran a business in Beijing that sold locally made specialty products to a well-heeled Western clientele. She vented that mainlanders don't "have pride in their craftsmanship or pride in their work." With comic outrage, Ellen recounted a recent situation in which a local supplier changed the color of her product labels without asking her. "I'm like, 'The color changed?' He's like, 'Yeah, *chabuduo*.' I'm like, 'No! I can't sell the same thing with a different color!' He's like, 'Yeah, but *chabuduo*.' It's not *chabuduo*! You know? But that's just the way people think. 'Whatever, good enough.' So, I think there lies a certain lack of professionalism."

Similarly, David, a media production assistant, also defined taking pride in one's work as a uniquely American quality. He linked this to the ideology of unlimited upward mobility through individual effort that underlies the American Dream. In the United States, he stated, "there is just a sense of pride in work. I think that comes from the American sense of individualism. . . . There's this idea that if you work hard at it and you show us something good, then you'll advance, whereas the Chinese colleagues that we work with have an attitude [of] *chabuduo*. It's good enough."

Some believed that, unlike Americans who maintain an ideal of upward mobility, mainlanders view social status as fixed and unchangeable, leading to a sense of complacency. Filmmaker Kevin candidly expressed that "you really just have to oppress your power upon [Chinese] people to get something done because if you [give them] the freedom to choose their own work, they're going to do the least required." He linked work performance in each society to the notion of equality: "Equality is a very American idea. In China, there's no equality. I would say [people here have] a very fatalistic view of the world. There's very little equality in general. At least in the States, people believe in the idea of equality. When you believe in the idea of equality, you will treat each other differently. No matter how much discrimination or class differences there are in the States, when people think about each other, they still see each other as equals, as human beings. In China, the biggest difference is that people don't think that at all."

ABCs tended to describe American workers in glowing terms, lauding them as workaholics who constantly strive for excellence and self-improvement. Sophia, who earned an MBA from a top U.S. program before joining a Western start-up in Shanghai, said that she had lowered her expectations of local employees. She viewed the differences in terms of personal initiative and internal motivation:

> The level of professionalism [here] is just very, very different. . . . In the U.S. I worked in consulting firms where people were generally very type A, were very responsible, and [were] very ambitious [whereas] locals are just looking for a stable job that pays them well, will pay their health insurance, a stable job that will allow them to save up money to buy a house or a car. . . . No stress. They don't necessarily care much about learning new things or development. They just want an easy job. A lot of locals want to try [to] get away with the least possible. They're not proactive. They just sit and wait for you to give them instructions instead of asking "Is there anything else I could do?"

Others, such as corporate health-care consultant Michelle, believed that the *chabuduo* mentality was a consequence of the PRC's incomplete infrastructure. Rather than framing it as a problem, Michelle was one of the few who suggested that this work style actually conveyed positive Chinese cultural qualities of ingenuity and practicality: "Because of the amount of work that has to be done, you [just] try to get something done as opposed to perfecting it. Like, we're not in Japan. You don't have an infrastructure already to produce the perfect product. [Here,] if this thing fits and it has a function to it, you use it. . . . You have to get where you can, and you work with it and get the experience. You build the capability, and then once you have more people, more hands on-board, then you try to improve it and onwards. That's the Chinese way. . . . They do what they can."

Working in a less linear, improvisational environment that prioritizes function over quality is also a frustrating experience for high-skilled ancestral homeland migrants in India. Similar to *chabuduo*, the second-generation Indian American professionals Sonali Jain interviewed complained about *chalta hai*—a Hindi term that refers to "a laidback and lackadaisical attitude" toward work in which "everything is acceptable, even when it is not."[19] Indian Americans also equated this attitude with a lack of professionalism, especially regarding time management and promptness. Jain quoted Ajay, a financial analyst for an American subsidiary in Mumbai, whose words closely echo the sentiments of his counterparts in China: "A lot of the people here have a very different way of thinking; they have the *chalta hai* attitude," he stated. "I'm American in this regard. I have a strong work ethic and sense of professionalism."[20]

In both the Chinese and Indian cases, the ancestral homeland migrants who felt most frustrated were those overseeing entry-level employees with less education and international experience. Most of these Asian American professionals imported Western ideologies that equated the commitment to one's job and work performance with personal character. However, as Jain aptly points out, punctuality, efficiency, and consistency "are not necessarily 'American' work characteristics but more a part of a global corporate culture" that demands these qualities from a highly skilled labor force.[21] Because ABCs generally viewed *chabuduo* as an essentialized Chinese cultural trait, they glossed over the inefficiencies and complacency that also exist in the U.S. workforce. Their approach to work reflected their high levels of educational attainment and professional training that correlate with global privilege.

To be fair, a number of ABCs also spoke with admiration about their well-educated Chinese colleagues, whom they lauded as being extremely diligent, hard workers. Individuals such as Michael, who worked at a Shanghai-based tech company, acknowledged the prevalence of the *chabuduo* mindset while also pointing out the incredibly strong work ethic that many high-achieving mainlanders possessed. "People here work like crazy!" he commented. Describing his local colleagues as "smart and hungry," he called them "very talented, very hard-working [and one of the main reasons] why China's rising so quickly."

GETTING LOCALS TO THINK OUTSIDE THE BOX

In addition to the *chabuduo* mentality, ABCs also commonly complained about what they saw as the lack of analytical thinking and problem-solving skills among mainland Chinese. Again, they identified these traits as quintessentially American and took it upon themselves to mentor local colleagues and subordinates. Jason, a forty-year-old Californian, had moved to Beijing thirteen years earlier and established several wildly popular restaurants. He lauded American individualism as a primary factor in his entrepreneurial success. Jason set himself apart from mainlanders, whom he scorned as unable to think for themselves. Expounding from his lavish living room, filled with imported white marble, he scoffed: "I'm always very, very, very critical of the way Chinese do things. One major thing that's helped me a lot in business is the fact that Chinese people are very uncreative. And so, in that sense, if your neighbor goes out and buys a black Audi A6, the average Chinese person would think, 'He got a black Audi A6, [now] I want a black Audi A6.' And for me, I'm like, 'If he bought a black Audi A6, that's the last car I want to buy!'" Jason described how he combated this attitude among his local staff: "Every time I have management meetings, one of the major [things I encourage is] 'be an individual. Try to shine!' This is something you [very much] learn . . . as an American. You want to stand out from everybody else. You don't want to be somebody else; you want to be yourself. So the Chinese people don't get that! They have no idea about that."

Respondents blamed the local educational system for inhibiting creative thinking, promoting hierarchical relationships, and preventing workers from taking more initiative. One individual characterized Chinese education in terms of collectivity, with the goal of creating a group "that will fit into society and the society's needs versus a system that fosters individual growth." ABCs believed that the Chinese emphasis on rote memorization inhibited critical thinking skills, which they then had to battle in the workplace.

Jeff, a journalist for a major U.S. news organization in Beijing, viewed this issue through a political lens, opining that the local educational system was an extension of the Chinese government's desire to keep its citizens complacent and unquestioning. Jeff contrasted this with the "American" style of critical thought. "There's a heavy dose of ideology that's implanted in the Chinese educational system [and] the idea of really critical thought about every aspect of life" is missing in the PRC, he stated. "If you have advanced education in the U.S., it's ingrained in you that you should be questioning everything in the media, everything you're told by your government, everything you're told by your parents. . . . When I get deeper and deeper in[to] conversations with Chinese, you realize there's a limit to that. For a lot of people, I do believe it's the way their educational system is set up."

Chinese American professionals were also extremely critical of the top-down, hierarchical structure of local workplaces, which placed total responsibility onto the shoulders of leaders. Kelly reflected on her time as manager of a number of young local employees at her foreign-owned media company. Americans, in her view, tend to "work at a certain level. We all feel this weird responsibility or obligation that we have to finish our task on time. And we're willing to figure out on our own how to do something." Kelly believed that her subordinates were simultaneously very talented and complacent, viewing this issue in terms of cultural differences: "I feel like in Chinese culture it's different. Like [local workers will] do things really quickly if you tell them exactly how to do it. If you tell them step by step, they probably can do it ten times faster than I can find in the U.S., right? But then you have to really tell them step by step. I think the most frustrating thing is that when they hit an impasse, they won't say anything. They'll just be like 'Oh, I can't do this task; it's not meant for me to do.'"

In another example, Cindy had been working in corporate management for a French-owned cosmetics company in Shanghai for several years. She brought an American management style to her job, flattening hierarchies and developing individuals' talents. When we met, she was managing a team of fifteen employees with 0 percent turnover—notable in a field in which workers tend to switch jobs every year or two. Cindy believed that her more diplomatic American approach was the key to her success: "I've been able to keep everyone that's on my team, and I think . . . it's my very American style. Because for me it's very important that you work hard, but [also] have a team spirit and a team dynamic. Plus, for me it's not just 'you do what I say' but 'I want to develop you if you have potential.' So I'm very clear in terms of my expectations of them, in terms of knowing what they want, understanding their needs, and helping them to grow. They may work hard, but they feel like they're working towards something, working towards developing themselves, so [the] team dynamic is fantastic."

Cindy elaborated on the difficulty of challenging local hierarchical structures. Like many others, she brought these issues back to a difference in educational systems. "The way we're brought up in the States, we're a lot more outspoken, we pose questions, and we have to think outside of the box," she remarked. "But in China, when they go to school, they're taught to memorize things, and so a lot of times they don't think the same way we do. So that's a lot of the challenges we run into."

In each of these cases, ABC professionals credited the U.S. educational system with teaching them efficiency, proactivity, and analytical thinking skills. In doing so, they revealed a blind spot toward pervasive differences in American levels of educational attainment. According to a 2017 U.S. Census Bureau report, only one-third (33.4%) of all American adults had earned a four-year college degree. Of that group, 9.3 percent had a master's degree, 1.5 percent had a professional degree, and around 2 percent had a doctoral degree.[22] By contrast, all but one of my respondents had earned a bachelor's degree, 25 percent had a master's degree, 17 percent had a professional degree, and 5 percent had a PhD. By viewing work styles in purely cultural terms rather than as indicators of larger-scale differences in privilege based on citizenship, class, and global access to resources, ABCs reinforced social and economic hierarchies that justified the increased opportunities they enjoyed in the ancestral homeland.

Conclusion

Overall, my interviews suggest that China's rapid global rise has provided unparalleled career opportunities for highly skilled second-generation ABCs. According to Takeyuki Tsuda, later-generation diasporic subjects from industrialized countries have less economic incentive to return to ancestral homelands because "the desire to reconnect with their ethnic roots and explore their cultural heritage seems to be a stronger motive compared to ethnic return migrants from poorer, developing countries."[23] This was not the case for my participants. It may have been true for them in young adulthood, but after entering the career stage of the life course, ABCs were far more motivated to head east for the possibility of financial gain than for cultural connection.

Few individuals—even those who were born in China— expressed a deep feeling of emotional connection or sense of social responsibility to the country, which differentiates this population from other groups of Asian American ancestral homeland migrants. As I have shown, my respondents occupied a socially ambiguous space and consciously used their in-betweenness for professional benefit. Combined with the lack of Chinese state efforts to incentivize the involvement of later-generation Western-born descendants, they could use others' assumptions about their ethnic belonging and cultural knowledge to further their own careers.

Being considered primordially linked to Chinese culture by both locals and non-Chinese Westerners allowed ABCs to leverage strategic in-betweenness despite not fully comprehending cultural nuances. In that sense, they used assumptions about their ethnic belonging as a form of social capital in the ancestral home-land; in consciously orchestrated performances, they presented themselves differently depending on the audience and desired outcome. The only exception to this was Howard, the psychologist who felt indebted to contribute to the development of Chinese society. By contrast, the words of twenty-five-year-old Kathy, a social entrepreneur in Beijing, sums up the more typically individualistic approach espoused by many ABCs who pursue careers in China: "From a self-development point of view, I have a much better sense of what type of life I want," she asserted. However, "from the perspective of contributing to China or making any kind of contribution, period, I would say I honestly don't think so."

Seemingly unaware of how their elite social status and educational attainment has shaped their views of work, these professionals often reduced locals to unthinking automatons incapable of meeting high standards or creative problem-solving. By promoting so-called American characteristics of professionalism, a strong work ethic, critical thinking skills, independence, and self-motivation, ABCs reinforced the American Dream ideology in the ancestral homeland. Nonetheless, as chapter 4 will explore, the automatic advantages and high social status enjoyed by Chinese Americans in the PRC for the past few decades have been tempered by elevated expectations of their performance as well as growing competition from a large wave of high-skilled, Western-educated Chinese returnees.

4

Perpetually Chinese but Not Chinese Enough for China

The story of Victor Zheng, a Chinese American social media personality, exemplifies the challenges that emerge when American-born Chinese are subjected to narrow assumptions about Chinese ethnic identity and belonging. The clean-cut millennial from Virginia moved to Beijing after college to attend a language program at Tsinghua University in 2016. While there, he teamed up with a white expatriate friend named Dylan Lynch to form the singing duo Dylan and Vic. They quickly gained notoriety by performing covers of Chinese pop songs. After one video garnered nearly four million views on Weibo, the young men attempted to secure a local record deal. Negotiations fell apart when mainland entertainment executives demanded that Victor present himself to the public as a native Chinese rather than Chinese American.

As this book has explored, the term "American-born Chinese" (*meiji huaren*) is an ambiguous—and often misunderstood—social category in the ancestral homeland. Because mainlanders view China as the center of cultural authenticity for Chinese descendants, they often lack a clear understanding of what it means to be a Western-born, Western-raised Chinese person in China. Being Chinese is perceived as an all-encompassing master identity in which race, ethnicity, and nationality are conflated. As I have argued throughout these pages, there is little room to accommodate the far more complex lived experience of anyone who has grown up with a hybrid cultural identity.

In a lengthy self-produced YouTube video, Victor recalls the immense pressure that was placed on him to hide his identity as an ABC. Although executives acknowledged, in his words, his "talent, creativity, and the looks for media," they nonetheless doubted local audiences would accept him as anything other than Chinese. In the video, Victor fixes his steady gaze on the camera. Switching easily between Mandarin and English, he describes the limitations of being in-between Chinese and American in the PRC: "If I am pure Chinese, then Chinese audiences can rally behind the fact that I am a local Chinese with talent that speaks good English. [But] if I had a 'foreign face'—meaning not Asian—I would be able to attract audiences because foreign faces still have an element of exoticness about them in this market. As a *huayi* [overseas Chinese], we are neither foreign enough nor Chinese enough."[1]

Having spent only three years of his life in China—all in adulthood—Victor felt it would be grossly deceptive and inauthentic to completely deny his American background, education, and overall worldview. A blog post he authored opines that overseas Chinese who do not conform to these limited social expectations run the risk of offending locals. "Regardless of cultural background or what kind of experiences I may have had," Victor writes, "the fact that I am ethnically *Han* will always fix my identity as Chinese."[2] Taken together, he senses that mainlanders simultaneously envy ABCs and also pity them for identifying as American—an act equated with losing touch with one's ancestral roots or even betraying "the Chinese race."[3] Ultimately, Victor chose to end his singing career to stay true to his own sense of self.

This chapter explores the idea that due to simplistic assumptions about blood ties, ethnicity, race, and nationality in China, "ABC" is not seen as a meaningful or legitimate identity in the ancestral homeland; rather, it is considered one of many different groups of Chinese people. In the case of my respondents, who enjoyed myriad benefits of strategic in-betweenness in the workplace and beyond, being expected to competently perform

Chineseness on a regular basis created a host of challenges that their white expatriate peers could avoid. The Chinese Americans I spoke with discussed the stress they experienced from attempting to meet high local expectations of speaking flawless Mandarin; displaying a deep, nuanced understanding of local culture and history; and expressing a strong emotional connection to their ancestral homeland. Compounding these limitations, over the five-year period I conducted research, it became increasingly apparent that the advantages once enjoyed by these ABC professionals had begun to wane. They found themselves being replaced by a wave of talented, Western-educated *haigui* returnees who were far more literate in Chinese cultural and business practices.

Dealing with "Where Are You From?"

Whether in the United States or China, ABCs face questions regarding their familial origins that point to underlying assumptions about their perpetual Chineseness. As chapter 2 discusses, mainstream white U.S. society generally regards Asian Americans as "forever foreigners," making no distinction between recently arrived immigrants and American-born later generations.

Michael, a creative arts director from the East Coast, addressed this issue when we met in a Starbucks in downtown Beijing: "In the States, people always ask me, 'Where are you from?' And it wouldn't be about what state I'm from or what city I'm from. They want to hear that I'm Chinese." Michael described a conversation from his college years with an elderly white man in Los Angeles: "He's like, 'Where are you from?' I was like, 'Oh, I'm from Connecticut. . . . I go to school here in California.' He's like, 'No, no, where are you from?' And finally I figured out what he was asking and then said, 'Well, my family's Chinese.' I said I was born in New York. He's like, 'How come you don't have an accent?' I'm like, 'What type of accent?' And I thought he was talking about some sort of English accent, but no, really, he was expecting just because I had an Asian face that I would have some sort of broken English."

The child of two prominent Chinese-born scientists who were raised in Taiwan before moving to the United States to pursue PhDs, the Stanford alum had worked in Shanghai and Beijing for the last six years. Michael continued to describe his lived reality of in-betweenness in the PRC. "I am a product of my experiences, and those span across cultures, right? In the States, people want to hear that I'm Chinese, [but] the same thing happens here [in China]: 'Oh, where are you from?'" he reflected. "There's always a level of comfort when they hear you are from somewhere that they might suspect, 'Oh, *meiji huaren*, right? You're Chinese American.' And then things sort of click. So, for me, no matter where I am, I'm not 100 percent a part of the place, but I'm somewhere in-between."

My participants generally concurred that back home, being asked where you are from demonstrates cultural ignorance at best and racism or xenophobia at worst. Yet as Michael's comment implies, they were actually asked this question more frequently in China; this caused them to develop strategies to manage similarly simplistic Chinese assumptions about their racial, ethnic, and cultural identities. During their first few months of living there, many reported a process of trial and error in which they perfected both short and long versions of their origin story, which they would deploy depending on context. These interactions reinforced the fact that these transplants, having Chinese heritage, would never be considered legitimate foreigners (*laowai*)—regardless of how out of place they actually felt.

Monica, a thirty-four-year-old advertising executive, recalled being unprepared to constantly have to explain her origins to local people after she moved to Shanghai three years earlier. "In the beginning it was just kind of entertaining," she mused. "I would tell them that I'm from America and they would go, 'But you don't look American at all; you look really Chinese!'" Monica quickly realized that most mainlanders subscribed to the overarching belief, informed by U.S. sitcoms and Hollywood movies, that all Americans were white people with blond hair and blue eyes. These conversations tended to be circular, ultimately ending with them defining her as Chinese. She recounted: "[Locals] were just really curious and interested, [a] 'Wow, you're from America? How did that happen?' kind of thing. And they would just continue to ask me a lot of questions. And then you have to explicitly tell them . . . , 'My parents were originally from China and went to the U.S., and I was born there and that's how I became American.' And they are like, 'Oh, so you *are* Chinese then; you were just born there!'"

Because Americanness is equated with foreignness, and foreignness is equated with whiteness, in the PRC, most of my interviewees found it easier to identify themselves as Chinese American. According to Stephanie, who had lived in Shanghai for over three years, locals always categorized ABCs as Chinese because they could not distinguish among race, culture, and nationality. With exasperation, she explained her way of dealing with constantly being asked about her origins by taxi drivers (whom she and many others equated with "your average local" due to their high frequency of interactions):

> To be honest, I just want to say something and then have them shut up. Because every time I get in a taxi, I don't want to go through this again, so I just say *meiji huaren* [Chinese American] and that's the end of the conversation. But if I said *meiguoren* [American], they'd be like, "Oh, really?" Like, I don't think they would understand it. *Laowai* [foreigner] to Chinese really means white. . . . So I feel like when [you call yourself] *meiguoren*, you're challenging a Chinese assumption of what a *meiguoren* should be, and it's just too complicated. You're taking a position. Because I'm not *meiguoren* to Chinese people, there's no way.

It is important to note that despite often referring to working-class male taxi drivers in their anecdotes, the ABCs I spoke with generally believed that the vast majority of Chinese natives—regardless of their socioeconomic class or educational background—view Chinese Americans as Chinese. At the same time, three people in my sample chose to identify themselves first and foremost as American. For instance, Charles, who had moved to Shanghai three years earlier, did so because he equated ethnicity with nationality. We sat outside in metal chairs on a side street in the French Concession, watching the bustling traffic pass by. "If [the conversation] is just really short, then I'm American, from North Carolina," he reasoned, leaning forward for emphasis. "It just boils down to the fact that I have only one passport." The twenty-six-year-old admitted that this approach invariably led down a winding path of follow-up questions about his family's migration history. His basic curt reply: "I'm American, my parents are from Taiwan, and then my grandparents are from China."

As we have seen, my respondents' reasons for relocating to the PRC were primarily economic and career related; very few equated their move with returning to an emotional homeland. Yet the common belief among mainlanders that China is the core of cultural authenticity and belonging for the entire global diaspora automatically led them to assume that ABCs moved there out of a deep yearning for the motherland. Paul was an outspoken former social activist who was born in Taiwan and grew up in California. After living in Beijing for nearly a decade, he was well versed in conversations with locals about his origins. Like millions of other overseas Chinese, his personal history had been complicated by the Chinese civil war, from which his father's family fled from China to Taiwan in the 1940s.

Paul was dressed in all black and appeared much younger than his forty years. He sipped his coffee and quipped, with comic timing: "[Locals are] always like, 'Oh, so you came back!' And I say, 'No, I never came from here.' And then, 'Where are you from?' And I say, 'Well, I was born in Taiwan.' And [they say,] 'Oh, you're Taiwanese!' And I say, 'No, I'm not Taiwanese. . . . My dad is from China. He was born in Shanghai. My mom was born in Taiwan.' And they're like, 'Well, where were you born?' 'Taiwan.' 'Oh, then you're Taiwanese!' 'No.' It's not that easy, but I think it's just [that] people don't have a reference point for this type of thing here."

I also spoke on the phone with Matthew, a venture capitalist who had lived in Beijing and Shanghai for a decade, as he fit our conversation into a hectic schedule of meetings with local partners. A Chinese major in college, he provided an overarching, scholarly interpretation of why locals automatically view ABCs as Chinese: "The big elephant in the room is what constitutes your Chinese identity, right? There's China the country—the geopolitical entity—and then there's being Chinese ethnically, and then being Chinese culturally. And being Chinese culturally can mean being mainland Chinese, Taiwanese, even Hong Kongese, Singaporean, [or] Chinese American." In these ways, most mainland Chinese citizens automatically conflated shared ethnicity with shared culture in ways that rendered the hybrid identities of those who straddle nations virtually nonexistent.

The Limits of In-Betweenness: The Downsides of Perpetual Chineseness

Despite the many professional opportunities enjoyed by ABCs, these comparative advantages were nonetheless limited by their cultural incompatibility with Chinese-managed workplaces. They described the challenges of meeting overly high expectations that native Chinese people had of their Mandarin-language skills and cultural knowledge. The most successful of my respondents were generally either entrepreneurs or employees of multinational companies; strikingly, none worked for local Chinese firms.

Several individuals I met began their time in the PRC in positions with Chinese companies before quickly moving on to jobs in Western-style environments. In their view, having shared ethnicity paved the way for mainland bosses to "treat them like locals," which they associated with negative aspects of work: minimal praise, lack of work-life balance, and not honoring contractual agreements. Twenty-nine-year-old Lisa, a finance executive, worked as a headhunter for a local company for four months after arriving in Beijing. Over lunch on a humid early summer day, she described various reasons why she left her Chinese workplace: "My boss was very Chinese. She would always put you down every day, [which I realized was] a cultural thing. They don't ever praise you for something good you do. They always say you've done something bad so that you can improve. . . . Then I was required to work overtime a lot. And I realized it was because that's how they measure how hard you work, by the amount of time you put in, not so much your results. . . . It was very strange. Then the salary that we had agreed on was not kept. I realized contracts don't really mean anything here. Yeah, so it was kind of hard working for that company here."

Monica, a thirty-three-year-old advertising executive who first moved to Shanghai for a position in a Chinese firm, echoed the challenge of not receiving positive reinforcement, something she believed to be an inherent—and highly motivating—aspect of American workplaces: "Whenever I did do something well, I wasn't shown any sort of appreciation or any kind of acknowledgment, whereas that was something that I came to expect from working in the U.S. It's like you get a pat on the back, and it was kind of an affirmation that fueled me . . . so it was just a very sort of negative kind of experience." Monica also complained about the long hours expected of Chinese workers, even though, in her view, her colleagues were very inefficient. "Everyone worked overtime all the time, as if they had nothing else better to do outside of work," she recalled, "and so they would just stay and work. And then I almost felt bad for leaving at 6:30." Desperately unhappy, Monica left the company after only two months, finding a more suitable position for her temperament with a multinational organization.

My respondents were often aware that due to different cultural expectations of work, they were less able to leverage strategic in-betweenness within local companies. For instance, Joy, an e-commerce executive, took pride in her outspoken nature but was also aware of how being opinionated limited her professional options in China: "My competitive advantage only occurs when I work for a multinational company. I can never work for a local company because I don't know how to read between the lines and can't be very direct with the boss and just [have to agree] with what he says. . . . It's only advantageous if I stick within the world I understand."

ABCs also continually compared themselves to their white expatriate peers and perceived these "legitimate" Westerners as accruing distinct advantages. Although looking Chinese was often highly advantageous in terms of blending in and gaining trust, on the flip side, looking Chinese also meant lacking foreign cache. Stephanie, a writer in her mid-thirties who worked for a Shanghai-based PR agency for a year before starting her own business, believed she was seen as less important than her white colleagues. Speaking in a crowded bar filled with chattering expats, she described feeling some professional discrimination over her Chinese background and appearance. "The white faces were often invited to important meetings more," she grumbled, "because from a client perspective, it's like, 'All right, this company is international. They've got a white face at the table.'"

EXPECTATIONS OF LANGUAGE FLUENCY AND CULTURAL UNDERSTANDING

Unlike their non-Chinese expatriate peers, ABCs were held to high standards regarding their skills in Mandarin. For instance, Jonathan was a corporate lawyer in Shanghai who grew up speaking Chinese and had further developed excellent language skills while living there. We talked in one of the conference rooms in his downtown office. Impressively dressed in a navy-blue tailored suit, crisp white shirt, and polished black leather loafers, Jonathan conveyed a quiet authority. However, he spoke of the drawbacks of being in-between in terms of unequal race and culture-based criteria that could negatively affect perceptions of him at his firm. Although mainlanders "don't outright treat you with discrimination," he reflected, "a lot of people will look at you and say, 'You're Chinese. You should speak perfect Chinese!'" He compared this outsized expectation to that applied to his white American law partner: "[If] the white partner says some stuff in Chinese, everyone goes crazy. They're like, 'Oh, that's freaking awesome! Let's keep talking.' But if I say it, it has to be really good. [Either way,] (a) it doesn't elicit the same reaction, and (b) whatever I say is never good enough. It's not fluent. Whereas Chinese Americans are definitely able to navigate the system here better, and that's the advantage, the disadvantage is that we're just stuck in-between."

Brian, an amiable financial adviser who moved to Beijing after graduating from Princeton University, grew up speaking Mandarin with his family and visited relatives in China regularly as a child. Now in his mid-twenties, Brian was comfortable with the language and culture but also felt tremendous pressure to prove his abilities compared to those of white expats. "For someone who's white, if they manage to string together a sentence in Chinese, people are like, 'Wow. That's incredible!'" he proclaimed. "But if I can't read one word on the menu, people will look at me like, 'Whoa. What's wrong with you? Are you illiterate?' So, yeah, I mean, the expectations are much higher for me."

Interestingly, because Mandarin is the official language of the PRC, these elevated standards also applied to Chinese Americans who grew up speaking Cantonese (a regional dialect). Cantonese speakers squirmed under the pressure they faced from locals. I met Diana, a twenty-six-year-old woman who worked for a tech start-up, after finding her thoughtful blog about life in China as an ABC. Dressed casually in a yellow sundress and sandals, the slender young woman from Southern California described the linguistic challenges she faced upon arriving there nearly four years earlier: "Because I look Chinese, there's this expectation of language. But I think that's something that kind of pushed me to work harder to learn Chinese [Mandarin]. Because it was really frustrating that people would expect me to speak, and I couldn't speak, and they would almost look down on me. 'But you're Chinese; you can't speak your own language?' Even though, in my head, well, 'I'm Cantonese! I can speak Cantonese. I can't speak Mandarin.'" Polishing off a green salad, Diana connected these expectations back to simplified assumptions mainlanders made about her emotional ties to the ancestral homeland. "People would always ask me when I first came, 'What brought you back to China?' Which kind of threw me off, 'cause I had never been to Mainland China," she recalled. "In their head, it's like, 'What brought you back to your mother country?' So, people definitely see you as Chinese first, not American."

These expectations of language extend to all overseas Chinese diasporic groups and are often used to assess one's level of cultural authenticity. In their study of Singaporean Chinese in the PRC, Brenda Yeoh and Katie Willis found that "for those Singaporeans who were expected to speak Mandarin but spoke it poorly, Mandarin became a sign of racial and national shame."[4] Similarly, twenty-six-year-old George, who arrived with only an elementary level of Mandarin, struggled with the perceived moral implications of his language abilities. He humorously compared these outsized expectations to those of "Western" (that is, white) individuals: "When you're a Chinese American trying to speak Chinese, it's much harder than if you're Western. If you're Western, you can say literally three words and they'll be like, 'Wow, that's so impressive. I can't believe you learned Chinese, the world's hardest language!' And then, when I, a Chinese American, speak Chinese, they're like, 'You really have given up on your mother tongue, haven't you? You've really disgraced your heritage.'" Rather than being offended, George chose to take a conciliatory approach. Upon first meeting, he would lower others' expectations with an apology: "I'm sorry that my Chinese is not that great. Please teach me!" He found that by humbly admitting to his perceived faults, locals were more sympathetic and willing to engage with him.

EXPECTATIONS OF CULTURAL KNOWLEDGE

Previously I have discussed the numerous strategies ABCs used to capitalize on others' assumptions about their innate Chinese cultural and historical understanding. This also meant that they were held to far loftier standards than their white peers. As financial analyst Lisa explained, "There's a lot more pressure as a Chinese American to assimilate. You have to do it much faster, and you have to learn much faster [because of] higher expectations." Due to the conflation of race, ethnicity, and culture in China, mainlanders often expected ABCs to be familiar with *all* things Chinese. I met with Tony, a technical manager for an American video game company, outside his modernistic office building in Beijing. Casually clad in a graphic T-shirt and jeans, the lanky young man described growing up in a Mandarin-speaking household in Northern California. He laughed when recounting his local colleagues' unrealistic expectations about his knowledge of classical Chinese novels: "Sometimes people expect me to know more than I know [about] Chinese culture. . . . They'll ask me, 'Oh, haven't you read *Journey to the West* in Chinese, or haven't you read *Romance of the Three Kingdoms* in Chinese?' And I'm like, 'I've seen the cartoon. I've never read the original text because it's too hard for me!' And they'll be kind of surprised because they see me as Chinese."

In the workplace, ABCs were occasionally even shamed by Chinese coworkers over their gaps in cultural comprehension. Kelly, an entertainment executive, detailed the ways her company's local partners would openly berate her parents for not teaching her more about Chinese history—knowledge they viewed as integral for doing business in the PRC. Flipping back her locks of funky red-dyed hair, Kelly recalled a recent dinner banquet with a mainland collaborator who questioned her professional abilities in this way: "How can you do business in China? So much of what we do in China is rooted in our history, and if you don't know that, then how can you do anything related to Chinese culture?" He then followed up with a more specific challenge: "How can you *possibly* know what a good movie is in China if you don't know *all* of this other stuff?"

Kelly admitted that her knowledge was spotty and mostly derived from media she had consumed as an adult. However, she scoffed at the idea that one must be completely culturally fluent to do good business. Visibly annoyed, she recalled her thought process: "You guys all love watching American movies, but you don't grow up with American history or culture. You guys love it . . . for the same reasons that we do, and Hollywood has figured out a formula and marketing campaign that resonates with a global audience." She continued, "They feel like, 'Oh, you can't do business with me unless you know [history and culture] because you're Chinese and you're *supposed* to know this stuff.'"

In both overt and subtle ways, ABCs felt pressure to understand the finer nuances of local business culture. Amid a sea of largely nonintuitive social practices used to cultivate local relationships, those who worked closely with Chinese clients described engaging in a never-ending learning process. They needed to continually build the *guanxi* (social connections) that keep personal and business relationships in the PRC running smoothly. Sociologists Thomas Gold, Doug Guthrie, and David Wank go so far as to suggest that *guanxi*, which relies on continual reciprocity and performing acts that "give face" (*mianzi*) to others, is "absolutely essential to successfully complete any task in virtually all spheres of social life" in Mainland China.[5]

As a system of "reciprocal obligation and indebtedness," *guanxi* encapsulates the performance of personalized favors, gift exchanges, and sometimes the throwing of lavish banquets at which everything—from the seating arrangements to the courses (as well as the order in which they arrive)—is fraught with symbolic significance.[6] This complicated set of practices, according to Gold and colleagues, "perform a critical lubricating function" in Chinese social and business relationships.[7] Yet for ABCs who did not grow up with these customs, the entire system can be confusing and even alienating. Michelle, a health-care consultant, described the difficulties ABCs face in understanding and employing *guanxi*: "If you look Chinese, they would kind of treat you as one. What that means is if you meet with clients, or anyone, you are expected to act like [a native-born Chinese person]. So that means you have to know what the social norm is, the etiquette, the way of doing business, and all these kinds of things, which you sometimes don't know."

Ilene, who had worked in Shanghai for over a decade, recounted her own arduous process of learning how to build strong relationships with mainlanders. Even after many years, the forty-two-year-old admitted to still constantly making mistakes. Although the corporate executive was acclimated to local behavioral expectations, it remained challenging for her, as an American, to accurately perform *guanxi* with her social networks. She struggled with practices such as gift giving, which to her was a necessary but also uncomfortably instrumental business strategy. "I literally have a list in my phone of who I have to give gifts to," Ilene stated.

"And when I'm talking to someone, I will mark something in my head, 'Oh she just had a baby. It's May. I have to give a gift after one hundred days.' I'm always thinking that, whereas in the U.S., I would never even think that way. I would think about writing a thank-you note, but I'm never thinking about how to strategically give to people in the most opportunistic times."

Ilene attributed the highly personalized nature of business relationships in China to the lack of a comprehensive legal infrastructure, which, unlike in the United States, requires developing deep levels of trust before working together. She continually sought out ways to give gifts in a "deft manner" that could build relationships and express appreciation without appearing overtly transactional. Furthermore, she spent a great deal of time figuring out how to invite people out to dinner so that "it doesn't look like I'm trying to 'buy them,' but am trying to get to know them better." With a resigned shrug, she concluded, "It is an art."

Many second-generation Chinese Americans expressed irritation with these expectations. They felt pigeonholed as perpetually Chinese, though their lived experiences were far more complex and nuanced. As Michael noted proudly, "I am a product of my experiences, and those span across cultures. So for me, no matter where I am, I'm not 100 percent a part of the place, but I'm somewhere in-between."

Others took a longer-range historical view that helped assuage their frustrations. Steve, who had witnessed vast social transformations over nearly two decades of living in Beijing, viewed this issue more systematically. We spoke in his home as his two young children played across the room. China is "an ethnically homogeneous country, which was closed off from the rest of the world for an awfully long time," Steve pointed out. "Until two years ago, most people still lived in the countryside." Because of this, he argued, it was arrogant for ABCs to expect locals to understand the concept of bicultural identities. "Why would you expect it to be different? I mean, why would you expect [mainlanders] to understand this idea that race and nationality are separable?" he scoffed. "You know, not everyone is going to understand that. It's something that we take for granted as Americans. It's strummed into us from the time we are very young." Instead, he critiqued this view as a "really maddening superiority complex" that he felt many ABCs brought with them to China.

Most respondents felt that Chinese Americans were generally held in high regard in the PRC, with their U.S. citizenship, educations, professional achievements, and English language fluency placing them in a structural position that one person described as "the best of both worlds." Richard, a twenty-seven-year-old owner of a popular restaurant in Beijing, summed up the advantages he enjoyed as a result of having a Chinese face and good Mandarin skills. In his view, mainlanders considered ABCs "super entrepreneurial" and highly successful hard workers. "They're like, 'Everything [ABCs] touch is gold.' I've heard that from so many locals," he remarked. At the same time, Richard acknowledged that this positivity tended to rely on their conflation of Chinese Americans with *haigui* returnees: "They basically think that you went abroad, you got all this knowledge, and you just came back and you're doing what you're meant to be doing." Notably, he did not correct this erroneous assumption among his local business partners, making sure to never speak English around them to maintain the facade of cultural sameness.

Unlike Richard, twenty-eight-year-old filmmaker Kevin believed that local people often pity ABCs as *jia laowai* (fake foreigners), whose cultural authenticity has been diluted by the United States—another adverse consequence of being considered perpetually Chinese. To him, it boiled down to the fact that mainlanders divide people into only two categories—foreign or Chinese—which, as Victor Zheng's story demonstrates, are seen as wholly disparate. "A lot of local Chinese people see this sense of shame in being Chinese American," he opined, because they "are not really Chinese and they're not really American. In the local Chinese person's mind, being white means being American or being black means being American." Kevin elaborated on the issues this can create for ABCs who claim an American identity in the ancestral homeland: "In China, they think, 'Oh, you're not really American. You're just a Chinese person living in America.' When they see a Chinese American being really proud of being Chinese American, deep in their hearts they see a very pathetic Chinese person trying to be an American that they'll never be."

Of course, it is overly simplistic—perhaps even dangerous—to essentialize Chinese culture by assuming that all PRC citizens share the same rigid viewpoint. As philosopher Tu Weiming has written, "China, or Chinese culture, has never been a static structure but a dynamic, constantly changing landscape."[8] Individual perspectives are clearly shaped by generation, socioeconomic status, educational level, geographic location, whether or not they have traveled or studied abroad, and other factors. Furthermore, it is likely that this view is softening as the country continues to globalize and welcomes home millions of middle-class, Western-educated Chinese students who are returning to the country for good.

ABCS LOSING THEIR EDGE: COMPETING AGAINST *HAIGUI* RETURNEES

Being a Chinese American professional in Beijing or Shanghai was advantageous for my respondents, as long as they could maintain the role of cultural liaison at higher levels of management. Even so, nearly everyone I spoke with mentioned the palpable and rapid increase in strength, skills, and savviness of white-collar Chinese workers. Although in the past, many first-world professionals had to be lured to jobs in the PRC with "expat packages" that included a high salary, a housing stipend, and educational benefits for children, these lucrative offers have since become scarce and difficult to obtain. Repeatedly I heard that China's formerly insatiable desire for Western management and expertise was waning alongside the growing wave of highly skilled *haigui*—especially top performers who earned advanced degrees from prestigious first-world universities and gained impressive foreign work experience before moving back.

To give a sense of scale, one-third of all international students in the United States are Chinese, vastly outnumbering those from any other nation.[9] The majority are enrolled in graduate master's and PhD programs (32% and 15% of the total in 2018), though under-graduate and high school students have also increased quickly.[10] Over the past three decades, 80 percent of the more than five million Chinese students who obtained foreign degrees—not only from the United States but primarily so—have moved back to the PRC; this fact directly contradicts the notion held by many Americans that all immigrants to the United States seek to stay there permanently.[11] The 2008 global economic recession spurred a huge spike in returns due to limited career opportunities elsewhere. More recently, this trend has been exacerbated by the Trump administration's extreme trade tariffs against the PRC, anti-Chinese and anti-immigrant rhetoric, and delays in accepting student visas, which caused the Chinese Ministry of Education to take the unprecedented step of asking the country's students to reconsider studying in the United States.[12]

Western-educated mainlanders have clear economic reasons for returning home. Yet many also choose to move back for "cultural comfort" and the desire to be in a familiar linguistic and social environment.[13] National pride plays a role as well, as those who consider themselves loyal patriots and tend to agree with the Chinese government's decisions are more likely to repatriate.[14] Even so, some of my respondents expressed surprise that the United States was losing its allure as a permanent migrant destination. Sarah, a forty-year-old social science researcher in Beijing, viewed this issue through the lens of political freedom. She wrestled with the idea that *haigui* would rather live under an authoritarian regime than enjoy what she perceived as the benefits of Western democracy. "It disappoints me that the political situation [in China] doesn't seem to bother most people. It's like the whole idea of the freedom of the West doesn't seem all that enticing," she commented. "That's been a little disappointing because maybe I came here with a naive idea that our way is a better way. I still believe it's got its good points. I would've thought that more [Chinese] people would want to stay, but they actually want to come back because the lifestyle they can have here is not bad."

The influx of returnees has greatly affected the Chinese economy. A glut of overqualified workers has, for example, raised the unemployment and underemployment rates of Western-educated job candidates. One recent survey of more than two thousand *haigui* reported that 80 percent were earning lower-than-expected salaries, and 70 percent believed that their positions did not match their skills and experience.[15] As one scholar notes, "the lofty, high-paid positions that returnees once assumed were all but guaranteed are now elusive aspirations that are more difficult to achieve than ever before in China's highly competitive economic environment."[16] These new pressures have begun to crowd ABCs out of the market, as they compete with highly educated returnees willing to accept lower wages. These returnees also have the advantages of being more fluent in Chinese language and *guanxi* practices and have comparatively good English skills and wider nets of local social connections on which to draw.

Lily, a twenty-nine-year-old corporate lawyer, had lived in Beijing for five years after graduating from college. We chatted in her cozy living room in a newly built high-rise apartment in 2013. During our conversation, the young woman credited her professional success in China to good timing. Sitting cross-legged on her couch, Lily absentmindedly toyed with her long hair. "Chinese students are the biggest percentage of foreign students in the U.S. in higher education, and they're all going to come back here," she commented. "Once they come back, they're going to replace people like me, right?" But, she noted, "the one thing I have advantage-wise, I'm here already. I'm working already." Lily felt secure at her international law firm, though she predicted that "given another few years, [I won't] have [my] comparative advantage anymore." Indeed, within just two years, Lily had moved back to the United States to marry her longtime partner and accepted a high-paying position as an attorney for a major Silicon Valley–based company.

Numerous others mentioned that the advantages of being an ABC in China were beginning to slip. I met with David, a hip-looking media production specialist dressed in all black, in a crowded coffee shop near the Xizhimen subway station in Beijing. With six years of experience in the local entertainment industry, the youthful thirty-five-year-old was engaged to a local woman and had no plans of leaving. At the same time, David felt that his American upbringing limited his ability to comprehend cultural nuances in ways that affected his job performance. "In the workplace, then, I've found that just because you're ABC doesn't mean that you can understand and adapt to Chinese culture," he remarked, projecting his voice above the din of whirring espresso machines. "I think that's why there's a shift toward [hiring] somebody who really is Chinese, who is really born and raised here, who's gone and gotten some education from abroad and can bring it back." David was starting to feel as though he was at a professional disadvantage and mourned no longer being regarded as "special," compared to when he first arrived there in 2004.

Over the half decade I conducted interviews, more and more people mentioned that skilled *haigui* were replacing Western workers at all levels of management. My conversations with Alan, a gregarious, highly successful technology equipment sales director, reflected this progression. In the summer of 2013, we met at an empty Indian restaurant in Shanghai for lunch. Sporting a deep tan and wearing a loose neon-colored tank top, shorts, and flip-flops, Alan had just come from a weekly expat beach volleyball game. Between large bites of chicken tikka masala, he speculated that "the dawn of the age of the expat Chinese American or expat American coming to China . . . is closing." Pausing to wipe thick orange sauce off his plate with some naan bread, he quickly followed up: "I don't think we're there yet, 'cause I look at all the recruits that we have. I look for the best people. I still want to hire expat," he clarified. "I think the biggest benefit for expats or Chinese Americans comes just from communication. Say you're in your weekly meeting with the local guys here . . . and it's in English, and it's a refined presentation. Communicating so people feel comfortable investing in you—that's still hard for a local Chinese to come and do."

When we spoke five years later, Alan—now a forty-year-old father of two—admitted that the advantages for Chinese Americans were dwindling. In his view, *haigui* had become the most sought-after workers, followed by Taiwanese and Singaporean Chinese, and, only after that, ABCs. Alan had played an instrumental role in quadrupling his company's sales over the past three years. Yet he was astounded by the rapidly expanding abilities of his local colleagues, who were bringing a whole new level of expertise and vision to China. Although his position felt secure, Alan had nonetheless decided to enroll in a part-time Chinese executive MBA course to "sharpen [his] game," become more polished, and improve his already excellent Mandarin.

Among my most recent interviews in 2018, one prominent theme that emerged was the need to maintain a competitive edge as companies shifted toward hiring returnees over ABCs. Roger, who worked as a manager for a Western beverage company in Shanghai, was trying to improve his professional skills as well. Despite having earned an MBA from a top-ranked American university, he was experiencing a growing sense of panic. "I know I only have a little bit of time to upgrade my local language skills or understanding of how to do business in China," he explained. Roger used the metaphor of water to describe his feeling of *weijigan* (a sense of crisis): "I feel like the water level is always sort of rising. Right now, maybe the water level is at my neck, and I need to keep rising, upgrading myself, otherwise I'll just drown. . . . I know the pie is shrinking, so basically, I have to keep advancing. Otherwise, I'll be squeezed out."

The surge of talented returnees even pushed some ABCs out of China permanently. After working for eight years in Beijing, health-care consultant Michelle decided to transfer to her company's office in Singapore. We first met in 2013 and reconnected in 2018, just a few months after she had transferred again, this time to her company's Chicago-based headquarters. Michelle was now the mother of a toddler, and her move had been motivated by the desire to be closer to her parents and find more work-life balance. The successful executive reminisced fondly about her lengthy time in China and the incredible professional growth and opportunities she experienced there. Nonetheless, at age thirty-eight, she counted herself as part of an earlier generation of workers. She acknowledged graciously that her time in the ancestral homeland had drawn to a natural close with the arrival of many competent and "hungry" young *haigui*.

Michelle's child loudly clamored for her attention in the background as she listed off for me her reasons for leaving, despite her colleagues' pleas that she stay. "I didn't know how I would maintain my edge because of how fast . . . and how great the incoming talents were," she explained. "It's not like in the U.S., where you can probably stay around until retirement. It would be hard for people to replace you, based on your knowledge and experience. It's not so much the case in China." However, Michelle's sadness about moving away was mitigated by the global perspective she had developed over her years abroad; she considered this to be her most unique strength now that she had returned to the United States.

I also spoke with Jonathan in 2013 and again five years later. He and his boss were the only foreigners left in their international corporate law office in Shanghai. Over that short period, major transformations in the Chinese legal field had caused a plummeting in the need for Western input and expertise. His firm now preferred to hire talented *haigui*, about whom Jonathan said: "They went abroad, worked, went to law school, worked on Wall Street or whatever, and came back here." The changes at his company seemed to him symbolic of the PRC truly coming into its own as a global superpower. With a mixture of admiration and acceptance, he called *haigui* "the people who are going to rule the country for the next one hundred years."

Conclusion

Throughout this book, I have shown how essentialized understandings of race, ethnicity, culture, and national belonging in the PRC confer societal membership onto descendants. Although these core assumptions about the perpetual Chineseness of second-generation ABCs frequently served as a form of social capital, facilitating their ability to use strategic in-betweenness and often leading to rapid career advancement and greater opportunities, it was clear that they still benefited the most by working in the narrower area of entrepreneurship or in multinational corporations. Having a Chinese face and an American cultural identity was not always beneficial or understandable to local people, and it could create a range of limitations and disadvantages as well. Co-ethnicity was a double-edged sword in which mainlanders held ABCs to higher standards of linguistic ability and cultural understanding than they did their white expatriate peers. Another limiting factor was the large gaps in cultural awareness that individuals maintained regardless of how long they had lived in the ancestral homeland, which limited their ability to effectively practice *guanxi*.

At the same time, over the course of conducting this research, it became increasingly obvious that the positions once occupied by ABCs and other first-world workers were beginning to be transferred over to an elite group of high-skilled Western-educated *haigui*. In 2018, my respondents were especially concerned about "losing their edge" in the mainland Chinese economy, leading some to bolster their already impressive language and professional skills to avoid being pushed out. Others interpreted the entrance of new talent as a sign that their own professional trajectories in the ancestral homeland had come to an end. Furthermore, because most people were in their mid- to late twenties upon first moving to China, the decision to leave often coincided with other major life events, such as getting married or having children.

Ultimately for ABCs, the rigid, racialized divides used to separate insiders from outsiders, Chinese from Americans, and locals from foreigners come with major pros and, increasingly, major cons. As the PRC becomes more secure in its role as a global leader and invests in its most capable returnees, the ability of Chinese Americans to capitalize on their in-betweenness in the ancestral homeland has invariably diminished.

5

"Leftover Women" and "Kings of the Candy Shop"

The Gendered Experiences of ABCs in the Ancestral Homeland

"What is it like to be an ABC (aka an American-Born Chinese) living in China?" This question was posted anonymously on the popular question-and-answer site Quora.com. Thirteen men and one woman responded, providing lengthy answers about living and working as U.S.-born migrants in their ethnic homeland. Although the thread focused mostly on cultural identity and workplace issues, several male commenters alluded to their vastly increased dating options in China compared to the United States.

"Dating wise[,] perceived desirability goes up for most ABC males. Like anywhere else it depends on the individual, albeit most get a 'bump' in attractiveness," wrote one. Another warned his peers to keep their egos in check amid the copious amounts of flattery and attention of local women: "You may end up with a completely overblown and unrealistic self-image." However, he added, "As an Asian man from America, maybe that's karmic recompense." Chinese American women, some warned, do not experience the same increased romantic desirability as men, and in fact undergo a notable drop in attractiveness when they move to the PRC. Almost gleefully, one male poster addressed ABC women directly: "You find yourself measured against a totally different aesthetic in China. . . . That healthy tan looks lower-class suddenly, and those 'exotic' features that the white guys back home fetishized don't do a thing for you in China."[1]

Until now, this book has centered on the construction of identity and belonging among Chinese American ancestral homeland migrants. This chapter broadens this analysis by applying the framework of intersectionality—a theory of power that investigates how the intersection of varied social categories brings different advantages or disadvantages to groups and individuals.[2] In particular, I highlight the key role of gender and examine how it intersects with other salient categories of race/ethnicity, nationality, and social class to inversely shape the lives and trajectories of heterosexual ABC women and men in China.[3] As Chow, Segal, and Lin explain, "Individuals occupy intersecting positions in social structures. Those positions represent the socially constructed multiple inequalities of everyday life, an inequality regime in which diverse women and men are privileged or oppressed in many ways, sometimes simultaneously. Their positions afford them agency and options, but also impose barriers."[4]

Previously I have discussed the immense career growth and increased professional opportunities that both female and male respondents enjoyed as a result of their Western educations, language skills, cultural knowledge, and shared co-ethnic backgrounds. I found, however, that their paths deviated widely in their social and romantic lives, with heterosexual women's options being heavily constrained compared to those of heterosexual men. This was an unexpected reversal of their experiences in the United States, whereby Asian American women have long been sexually fetishized within mainstream culture while men have been emasculated through exclusionary race-based policies and negative media depictions.[5]

Relatively little attention has been paid to the gendered dynamics of privileged migration to East Asia.[6] The few previous studies of Western expatriate women in China have tended to focus on heterosexual married mothers; known as "trailing spouses," these women follow their "lead migrant" husbands abroad as they pursue job opportunities.[7] These mostly white, non-Chinese-speaking expatriate wives have a difficult time finding formal paid positions in the PRC. Forced to give up careers back home, they are relegated to the household and tend to have relatively sparse contact with local Chinese society. Their experiences are thus quite distinct from the mostly unmarried Chinese American professional women I interviewed, who proactively moved to Beijing and Shanghai to build their careers and were far more integrated into local gender dynamics.

Understanding the dating and marriage practices of heterosexual ancestral homeland migrants requires a closer examination of how they are affected by the local Chinese cultural context. By focusing on the social realm, I find that two conflicting yet coexisting approaches to gender shape the experiences of Chinese Americans there: the first is egalitarianism in the workplace (a legacy of Communist ideology), and the second is traditional patriarchal expectations of relationships. Despite comparatively high levels of workforce participation, urban Chinese women face intense pressure to marry early, bear a child, and possibly return to the home—objectives encouraged by the government in its pursuit of global dominance. In recent years, state authorities have even popularized the term "leftover women" (*sheng nü*) to stigmatize highly educated urban professional women who remain single in their mid- to late twenties.[8] Due to essentialized understandings of racial and ethnic belonging that are automatically conferred onto Chinese descendants, ABC women are lumped into this stigmatized group. By contrast, their male counterparts are precluded from this category, even though members of both groups typically relocate to China for work around the same age. ABC men's Western backgrounds and qualifications increase not only their professional opportunities but also their social status. This greatly expands their romantic options abroad.

In conjunction with a transient expatriate environment that favors relationships between foreign men of any age and beautiful young local women, female ancestral homeland migrants generally find themselves squeezed out of the local dating and marriage market. Whereas ABCs are able to opportunistically benefit from their cultural in-betweenness at work, this ambiguity creates diverse gendered outcomes in their social lives. Through using an intersectional approach to situate these high-skilled co-ethnic migrants within the local Chinese context, it is possible to see how power and privilege operate differently for women and men.

Gender Relations in the PRC

Before delving into specifics, it is useful to briefly highlight changes to Chinese gender dynamics since the nation's founding in 1949. The rise to power of the Chinese Communist Party (CCP) was fueled in part by its promise to eliminate institutionalized forms of oppression against women. The 1950 Marriage Law, one of the CCP's first major pieces of official legislation, sought to correct many long-standing systemic inequalities by giving women legal rights to property, divorce, and free choice in marriage. It also outlawed practices of "concubinage, child betrothal, multiple wives, and the sale of sons and daughters into marriage or prostitution," spurring a major wave of divorces.[9] Nonetheless, this vision of gender equality was, as scholars have argued, "doomed to failure," undermined by resistance from local officials and communities that were long accustomed to arranged marriages and patriarchal norms.[10]

In spite of resistance, the CCP continued to pursue gender equality through encouraging women's full participation in the productive sphere. Communist campaigns during the Mao era (1949–1976) promoted female inclusion in male-dominated work sectors. By 1958, the percentage of rural women involved in agricultural production had reached 90 percent.[11] Simultaneously, urban women entered into heavy industries such as construction; mining; and iron, steel, and petroleum production in unprecedented numbers. During the idealistic 1960s, characterized by Chairman Mao's famous phrase "women hold up half the sky," the CCP popularized propagandistic imagery of iron girl brigades:

female workers with strong physiques and youthful vitality who were held up as "models of a socialist future."[12]

These early efforts have achieved impressive, seemingly lasting results. The percentage of paid women workers in China is one of the highest in the developing world—roughly 61 percent in 2016, five percent higher than in the United States.[13] Despite very low representation within government ranks, women have found particular success as capitalist entrepreneurs. A 2017 study found that 49 out of 78 of the world's self-made female billionaires hailed from the PRC.[14] Zhou Qunfei, the founder of a company that produces glass covers for smartphones and laptops, sat at the top of the list. She was born in an impoverished village in Hunan Province in 1970, and less than fifty years later, her empire was worth an estimated US$9.8 billion in 2018—more than *triple* Oprah Winfrey's net worth.[15]

Individual successes notwithstanding, Chinese women have and continue to be constrained by patriarchal social expectations and "traditional" gendered roles in the home. Even during the socialist period—generally heralded as a golden era of gender equality—housework and childcare was not only unpaid but extremely undervalued. Like women in many industrialized countries, Chinese women were expected to devote themselves to their workplaces and then return home to perform a "second shift" of domestic duties, from which men were largely exempt.[16] Consequently, government efforts at the time "fell far short of enabling women to achieve autonomous agency or relief from their double burden at home."[17] State campaigns to instill gender equality at work did not transform the traditional household division of labor or marital expectations of subservience.

These dynamics have been exacerbated in the contemporary era. A resurgence of gender inequality in the urban workforce has reinforced the notion that women *belong* in the home. Census figures show that in addition to a widening gender wage gap, female employment in China's cities has plummeted from the high-water mark of the late 1970s (over 90%) to just over 60 percent in 2010 (more than 20% below men).[18] This trend overlaps with economic restructuring of the 1990s, by which millions of workers in state-owned enterprises lost their jobs through government privatization. Women's disproportionate firing and rehiring at far lower pay rates than men all but forced many to become housewives or contingent laborers. Furthermore, the dismantling of an employer-based social welfare system that had once provided paid maternity leave and subsidized childcare shifted most caregiving responsibilities to the family—and to women in particular.[19]

Sociologist Leta Hong Fincher links these sweeping changes to a propaganda campaign begun in 2007 that encourages female urban professionals to avoid becoming "leftover women" (*sheng nü*).[20] According to the Chinese Ministry of Education, this category includes "urban professional women who are over 27 years old who have high educational level, high salary, high intelligence, and attractive appearance, but also overly high expectations for marriage partners, and hence are 'left behind' in the marriage market."[21] Some claim that single women join this category as early as age twenty-five.

Sheng nü discussions place blame and responsibility on women's shoulders, asking them to limit their career ambitions and be less discriminating when choosing marriage partners. It is as if they are saying "lower your expectations or expect to be leftover." Although this line of thinking exists in Western societies as well, it is arguably more muted, especially within official government discourses. The dangers of being "leftover" are now the subject of myriad Chinese television shows, news reports, and academic research, invoking concerns that modern females are too educated, overly individualistic, and professionally successful to find a husband. In a time of unpredictable social change and a growing need for more skilled workers in the knowledge economy, this intervention into the intimate lives of middle-class women reflects broader Chinese state objectives to control the population and maintain a stable society.[22]

There have been some notable rebukes to this public shaming of China's unmarried career women. One unlikely source is the Asian skin-care brand SK-II, which produced a sentimental four-minute-long video about the social stigma of being "left-over." Viewed on YouTube nearly three million times, the short documentary features interviews with aging parents who interpret their daughters' single status as a sign of filial disrespect. As the camera pans over a dated photo of a smiling young girl, her elderly father declares in an emotional voiceover, "I won't die in peace unless you're married!" Another scene captures a woman in her thirties looking on tearfully as her mother, seated only a few feet away, describes her daughter as "just average looking. Not too pretty. That's why she's leftover." Other footage captures the huge outdoor Marriage Market held each weekend at People's Park in Shanghai, where hundreds of parents swap their children's information in an attempt to locate a suitable match.[23]

This intense pressure to marry is particularly striking because the *actual* numbers of single women are relatively low. According to a United Nations report, fewer than 10 percent of Chinese females in their thirties are single—far below the rates of other East Asian countries. In comparison, 22 percent of South Korean women, 28 percent of Singaporean women, and nearly 40 percent of Japanese women remain unwed in their early thirties.[24] Yet put into the broader historical context of the PRC, *sheng nü* reflects a socialist logic in which women's primary patriotic contribution lies in bearing and rearing productive laborers to enhance the nation's status.[25] Unlike in many industrialized countries, where educated women marrying later or not marrying at all can be considered empowering life options, in the PRC there are as of yet no "positive concepts for describing independent career women who do not fit into traditional domestic roles."[26]

This discourse is darkly ironic. China is currently facing an alarming *shortage* of women as a result of state-imposed fertility regulations—particularly the One-Child Policy, which was enacted between 1980 and 2015. Even though economic development has transformed most aspects of society, patriarchal emphasis on bloodline and the desire to bear at least one healthy son who can care for elderly parents has persisted, especially in rural areas. Facilitated by sex-selective abortion, this has resulted in the most extreme gender skew in children of any country in the world.

Scholars predict that by 2020, there will be roughly thirty million more males than females between the ages of twenty-four and forty in China, raising concerns about men's ability to find marital partners and continue their family lines.[27] Known as "bare branches" (*guanggun*), these men are generally poor peasants with limited education. They exist at the very bottom of the social hierarchy, where, instead of being leftover, they are being left behind by the forces of modernization. Hence, the marital options of both highly educated women and poorly educated men are extremely constrained. Despite the scarcity of females in China, this has not empowered women in regard to their romantic options, as might be expected. Because the composition of the population has changed far more quickly than patriarchal norms and ideologies, many women—including so-called *sheng nü*—now compete for the attention of a relatively small group of educated middle-class urban professionals. These conflicting local gender ideologies shape the social lives and trajectories of ABCs in the ancestral homeland.

Gender Egalitarianism at Work

As I have detailed, highly skilled ABCs often served as indispensable cultural liaisons between Western and Chinese business interests. My respondents used strategic in-betweenness by positioning themselves simultaneously as both cultural insiders and outsiders in the workplace, which gave them advantages over the locals and over non-Chinese expatriates. The combination of their elite backgrounds and shared ethnicity provided professional opportunities and rapid career growth in the PRC that appeared to surpass gender divides. Not only did respondents view gender as a nonissue in the workplace, many described their fields in terms of gender equity and women's advancement. Jonathan provided his perspective based on six years in an international law firm: "I don't feel like the women get any worse treatment here. As a matter of fact,

I think women in some senses have it better here than in the U.S.," he stated. "The[y make up the] majority of . . . our associates here—there are two guys and . . . twenty women. I'm on the hiring committee. Seriously, most of the people I interview that I like are women. They're just better qualified than men."

Due to their ability to fill key niches in developing Chinese economic sectors, over half of the respondents described experiencing rapid career advancement. Many women were offered opportunities and responsibilities that exceeded their age and experience levels. Jenny, a twenty-eight-year-old environmental consultant I spoke with in 2013, explained how she was uniquely positioned to benefit: "Promotion here happens very fast because there just isn't quite that level of mid-tier management yet that's capable of being international but also understand China. There's either very high-up people who own the companies or very junior people." She elaborated, "I'm still relatively low-level right now, but the idea [is that] if I work here for two to three years, I can get more into the middle level position faster, whereas if I was in the U.S., it may take longer."

Although the local ideology of gender equality in Chinese workplaces has benefited ABC women, they are doubly privileged by their American nationality combined with extensive U.S.-based education and training. Hence, this situation aligns with the notion of the ".edu bonus,"[28] in which Western-educated women's skills and training accord them more respect from colleagues when they work abroad. Many of my female respondents viewed the PRC in terms of unlimited career potential. As PR executive Christine exclaimed, "I do see a difference in terms of how fast [ABCs] accelerate here in terms of title and responsibilities. [China's] become in my eyes like a land of opportunity. Anything that you want to happen, it can happen."

Somewhat paradoxically, this perspective also reinforced the ideology of the American Dream—a gender-neutral space in which talent, motivation, and hard work can overcome external barriers to success. Many believed they could realize career objectives in the PRC in ways that were impossible in the far more mature American economy. I met with Michelle, a thirty-three-year-old health-care consultant, in Beijing's upscale Sanlitun district. We talked on metal benches outside a crowded Apple Store. For the past eight years she had worked her way up the ranks of her company and was now serving in a pivotal leadership position. Michelle, who we met earlier in the book, viewed her career trajectory through this lens of individual effort and merit-based achievement: "It's kind of a pretty level playing field for genders here. I feel like there's sort of equal opportunity either way as long as you have the talent and the passion to pursue whatever it is you want to pursue. I find that gender and age discrimination is more prevalent back in the U.S. as well as in many parts of Asia, with the only exception being China."

Her statement contrasted the PRC and its ideology of workplace egalitarianism with other East Asian countries reputed to have workplace cultures far less hospitable to women. For example, Helene Lee has discussed how second-generation Korean American women in South Korean workplaces consciously assert their American identities to challenge perceived chauvinism. The female workers she studied also contrasted the perceived gender egalitarianism of the United States with less than ideal gender dynamics in South Korea—a country they viewed as "constrained by traditional patriarchal attitudes and practices that left little room for successful women in the workforce."[29]

I asked Michelle whether she thought gender had played any role in her professional success. "It's about your capability!" she insisted, shaking her head rapidly. "The more capable you are, the more people will give you work. When I first joined my previous company . . . there was only $50 million worth of business. Within six months, my boss saw what I can do, and when I left at the end of two years I was leaving an $80 million business," she continued. "Just more opportunities were given to me. So at the age of thirty-three today, I'm doing a job that probably someone would have to be at least forty, probably fifty, in the U.S. to do." Her view, echoed by others, downplayed the privilege automatically conferred on her as a result of having American citizenship.

Kelly, a thirty-three-year-old high-level executive in a successful foreign-owned media company, echoed the rhetoric of equal opportunity. "In some ways it's easier to advance into positions of power in China as a woman than you can in the States," she mused. "I think the glass ceiling is far more difficult to break in the U.S. than China." At the same time, this perception of equal opportunity was contingent on having the right qualifications and adequate Mandarin skills. Notably, none of my respondents mentioned gender inequality or sexism as problematic issues in their Chinese workplaces. As chapter 3 explored, they did not encounter a "bamboo ceiling" like they had in the United States.

The Reversal of Romantic Desirability in the Ethnic Homeland

Among the single heterosexual Chinese American men I met, their language skills, citizenship, education, and typically higher-than-local salaries easily converted into social capital that boosted their local desirability for dating and marriage. By contrast, those same characteristics decreased the romantic appeal of their female counterparts with regard to *either* expatriate or local Chinese men. This phenomenon inverted many individuals' experiences in the United States, where the sexual desirability of Asian Americans has been constructed in distinctly racialized and gendered ways that lead to nearly opposite outcomes.

Exclusionary race-based legislation in the nineteenth century that severely limited the migration and incorporation of Chinese migrants into American society established narrow gendered stereotypes still influential today. Specifically, the Chinese Exclusion Act of 1882 and the Asian Exclusion Act of 1924 curtailed the entrance of Chinese women into the United States for several generations, relegating male immigrants to bachelor societies. Labor market restrictions also funneled many Chinese men into "feminized" jobs, such as laundry, domestic service, and restaurant work. In turn, past media representations of Asian American men have consistently portrayed them as hapless, asexual, or effeminate.[30] For example, the nerdy, heavily accented, socially awkward character of Long Duk Dong from the film *Sixteen Candles* served as the predominant stereotype of Asian American men throughout the 1980s. "Whether depicted as perverse, hypersexual, or effeminate," writes Stephen Cho Suh, "the masculinities of Asian American men have consistently been deemed suspect within the U.S. public imaginary, subject to various discourses of exoticism, criticism, and/or ridicule."[31]

On the other hand, Asian American women have been depicted as hypersexualized, superfeminine, highly desirable, and fully available to white men. Renee Tajima categorizes these media images into two main stereotypes: "the Lotus Blossom Baby (e.g. China Doll, Geisha Girl, and the shy Polynesian beauty), and the Dragon Lady (e.g. prostitutes and devious madams)."[32] Asian female characters are often "betrayed or exploited by men of their own race but are later saved by White male heroes."[33] Similarly, in the American media, Asian women have nearly always been cast as the love interests of non-Asian men. Although these images are changing, the ethnicized gendering of sexuality in American pop culture has reinforced the idea of Asian Americans as unassimilable Others, thus bolstering the power and superiority of white mainstream society.[34]

Today, these stereotypes measurably affect Asian Americans' romantic options. Numerous demographic studies of dating and marriage patterns in the United States have found that Asian women are considered more desirable and are more likely to marry interracially than are Asian men.[35] A 2015 Pew Research Center survey of newlyweds found that 37 percent of Asian women "married out," versus only 16 percent of Asian men.[36] Analyses of Internet dating data reveal that Asian women's profiles are generally rated highly by men of all races, whereas Asian men tend to be rated poorly by all women.[37] In fact, Asian women are far more likely to *completely exclude* Asian men from their online searches than they are to exclude white men: 40 percent versus 11 percent.[38] Whites are the least open to dating outside their group; nonetheless, of those who *are* open to it, 47 percent of white men would consider dating an Asian woman, while only 7 percent of white women would consider dating an Asian man.[39]

Among young adults, Asian American men—with the exception of Filipinos—have a much lower chance of being romantically partnered than men of other racial groups.[40] They are twice as likely as their female counterparts to be single (35% vs. 18%), which suggests a racial hierarchy of romantic preferences in the United States dating market.[41] Notably, this disparity eventually evens out when it comes to marriage, with only 12 percent of Asian men between the ages of forty and fifty reporting never having married, compared to 16 percent of white men. Overall, however, Asian men in the United States are perceived as less physically and sexually attractive than other men.[42] This situation completely reverses when they move to China.

ABC MEN'S EXPERIENCES OF DATING IN THE "WORLD'S LARGEST CANDY SHOP"

The romantic options of ABC professionals in the PRC were shaped by local gendered expectations of dating and relationships—issues that are exacerbated within transient expatriate communities. In addition to viewing the ancestral homeland as a place of cultural connection and career opportunity, some of the men in my study were motivated to move abroad to find a relationship. Richard was a thirty-six-year-old researcher who had lived in China off and on since his early twenties and married an East Asian woman he met during college study abroad. As a young man, he became aware of his more limited dating prospects in the United States, recalling, "I was noticing this disparity between mixed-race couples on the street. I was like, why is it always with the Asian females and not the Asian males in these relationships?" He added, "That kind of brought me down." Richard's decision to move to Shanghai in his early twenties was partly motivated by his hopes to "find a spouse."

Little is known about the romantic lives of Asian Americans in Asia. However, their experiences appear comparable to intimate relationships between white Western men and Asian women. Across East Asia, white men are hypermasculinized in ways that heighten their dating options.[43] Pei-Chia Lan's interviews with Western English teachers in Taiwan revealed, for instance, that men's geographic origins and English-language abilities deeply enhanced their social status and desirability. Indeed, many of her participants enjoyed "increased popularity in their romantic or erotic pursuit of local women in Taiwan in comparison to their dating experiences back home."[44] In his analysis of sexual relations between white men and Chinese women in Shanghai, James Farrer contends that men's "foreign masculinity" can be "both empowering and marginalizing," as it heightens their social status while simultaneously reinforcing their position as cultural outsiders.[45]

The dating and marriage practices of Asian male ancestral homeland migrants have been examined in Vietnam and South Korea, too. Like Richard, some Korean American men are consciously motivated to move to Korea to "recover a sense of masculine status and privilege denied to them as emasculated Asian-Americans in the United States."[46] Because they can leverage their Americanness as a form of "masculine cultural capital" that enhances their social standing relative to local men, young male Korean "returnees" experience vastly improved dating prospects in the ethnic homeland.[47]

This held true for the highly skilled ABC men I met, whose combination of Americanness, cultural knowledge, and co-ethnicity tended to work in their favor when dating in China. Individuals remarked on their dramatically increased status and desirability after moving there, which heightened their overall sense of self-confidence. David, a thirty-five-year-old media production consultant, remembered feeling marginalized and invisible growing up. After moving to Beijing in 2004, he was pleasantly surprised by his popularity among the local women. "Now I see in the [U.S.] media a lot more Asian Americans and all that, but back then I felt like there wasn't," he stated. "But when I came to China, it was like, 'Yeah!' People were interested in me. People would talk to me. Hey, man, girls were interested in me." David looked wistful as he continued, "I felt special . . . like I got more opportunities just because of who and what I am. ABC guys are like a hot commodity, you know? Whereas I think that in general, [ABC] women who come to China, they don't face the same set of opportunities."

David, who was cohabiting with his mainland girlfriend, described using his cultural in-betweenness to "charm" lovely local women. In his opinion, male ABCs benefited from the local view of Western men as being direct communicators and more respectful of women than PRC males while still having a Chinese face and shared cultural knowledge. He remarked that ABC men "come here and all of a sudden there are a bunch of beautiful girls kind of throwing themselves at you, you know? We charm them by being different."

Other men took a more structural view of Asian American dating trends. This included Steve, a tech manager in his mid-forties who was married to a woman from Beijing:

> Chinese American men don't have it all that good in America. There aren't a huge number of white women who have Asian male fetishes out there, right? So, the sexual power balance is different when Asian [American] men come here. They're suddenly in a sort of different position where they're actually more sought after, in part because of the passport, in part because of having a certain "worldliness." . . . Chinese American men come here, and they realize that they're at or near the top of the dating pecking order. It's a very different experience [for] Chinese American women, who end up mostly dating expatriates. You very rarely find Chinese American women coming here and dating local men, whereas you often find Chinese American men coming here, dating, and marrying local women.

Akin to white expat men, ABC men could find their new dating options to be overwhelming. Jonathan, a married father of two, described how this affected his single male friends in China: "It's kind of like they go crazy" with the women and the partying, "and so most single guys out here, whether they say it or not, I think they're living out some fantasy in that respect." Everyone seemed to know men who were juggling seeing multiple women at the same time—an issue that, while certainly welcomed by many, was nonetheless very time-consuming.

Playing the romantic field could even interfere with work. Benjamin, for instance, had spent a summer in China in his early twenties before returning to the United States for a decade to build his career. He married a Taiwanese American woman, and together they moved to Shanghai to open their own businesses. That was three years before we met one afternoon at the restaurant his wife Anna owned and operated. Benjamin believed that being married and not having to deal with the distractions of dating was key to his current professional success. "The dating scene is great if you're an Asian American guy! I mean, you have the expat background [so] locals love you," he enthused. "Expat girls don't date local guys, so you're very fought for! If I were to come when I was single, it'd be very hard to focus. Very, very hard to focus." Anna laughed, rolling her eyes as Benjamin continued: "Good thing I came married, otherwise I don't think it would work! My mind would be in other places."

Some Chinese American women derided their single male counterparts for developing "massive egos" that they felt were artificially inflated by the attention of beautiful young locals. Four separate women described China as a "candy shop" where Western men could—and were encouraged by their peers to—date casually or be sexually promiscuous without any negative repercussions. Regarding the ABC men she knew in Shanghai, single corporate executive Joy scoffed: "We always say it's like 'from zero to hero!'" She clarified that for men, "no matter who you are, if you come from the States you're like ten times more popular here. You're just perceived as more valuable." Although Joy acknowledged the limited dating options that Asian American men have back home, she disparaged their instantaneous popularity in China. "As soon as they come here, it's a playground, like a candy shop. All you can eat," she exclaimed. "If there's someone they like, most likely they can get them."

Sophia, another single woman, discussed this issue with me at length. She felt that the Chinese–expatriate social context caused ABC men to develop Peter Pan syndrome, in which "guys come here and just never grow up." Indeed, it was common to see foreign men in their forties pursuing local women half their age in clubs and bars—an observation echoed in Farrer's Shanghai-based study in which sixty- to seventy-year-old Western men commonly had Chinese girlfriends less than half their age.[48] According to Sophia, Peter Pan syndrome overlapped with the concept of "LBH" (losers back home), in which guys "who weren't that cool back home . . . come here and they're like demigods." In her view, most heterosexual foreign men passed through a "sleazy phase" of casual dating that generally either continued until they left or ended with marriage to a local woman. When I suggested that ABC men could reinvent themselves in China, she nodded, "Yeah, exactly. They're popular now. They're desirable now." Sophia sighed dejectedly. "I'm not bitter against guys or anything," she stated. "If I was a guy, I'd probably do the same thing. It's just the environment."

Both women and men mentioned major moral and ethical differences regarding casual dating and sexual relationships in the PRC compared to the United States. Specifically, they juxtaposed Judeo-Christian ideals of monogamy with local patriarchal norms in which men commonly engaged in extramarital relations. It was common to have a "second wife"/ mistress (known as *ernai*) or to solicit paid sexual services from hostesses and masseuses. Although prostitution is technically illegal in China, studies have shown that middle-class men's consumption of sexual services in hostess bars figures centrally in business culture—practices that Tiantian Zheng argues are often considered to be an integral part of a "modern" lifestyle. Business and sex go hand in hand as men "partake of the services offered by hostesses and at the same time engage in 'social interactions' that help cement 'relationships' with their business partners or their patrons in the government."[49] This more laissez-faire attitude toward casual sex and cheating permeates the expatriate social scene as well.

Twenty-five-year-old Steve was a single man working for a Western financial risk-management company in Beijing. His American citizenship, relative good looks, and height of six feet easily attracted female romantic interest. Steve described his time in China as a test of his ethical principles regarding the treatment of women. "I think as an expat here," he reflected, "especially from the male perspective, you go out anytime, and as soon as you start speaking English and people know you're from America, they tend to flock toward you." In a recent encounter, a local woman overheard him speaking English with a friend at Starbucks and eagerly introduced herself. Upon learning he was from the United States, she immediately suggested they hang out and offered her WeChat contact info. Some of these women, Steve believed, were truly interested in learning about the United States, while others were primarily "trying to get me to take them home." He tried not to pass judgment on the dating and sexual practices of his male expat peers, but Steve said their unrestricted behavior went against his own moral code. "I have certain friends who go to a bar on a Saturday night and they see three girls there that they have slept with, and it's like, 'Okay, wow,'" he remarked. "I have friends who wanted to go to those sketchy KTV [karaoke] places or massage parlors and it's like, 'That is not my scene. I respectfully decline.'" Steve noted that these experiences had clarified his own negative view of casual hookups: "I don't need to put notches in my bedpost. That's not what I'm looking for."

Despite the laxness of the surrounding environment, not all ABC men attempted to capitalize on their elevated social status to partake in casual flings. Like Steve, twenty-six-year-old George did not want to use his foreignness to attract women. Consequently, he did not date at all for the first three years he lived in Shanghai. By the time we met, he had been with his local Chinese girlfriend, whom he met online, for a year. Other Western men had advised George to "just speak English and you'll get the girl so easily," but the idea did not sit well with him. "I didn't want to [speak English to pick up women] because I'm Chinese," he said. "[And] if I speak Chinese, it's hard to hit on someone with a fourth-grade vocabulary. . . . [But] if you just speak English, you're going to get the girls who only want guys to speak English. And those are the girls I generally don't want to hang out with that much."

Having minored in East Asian studies at Harvard, George was able to place expat men's dating practices into a broader historical context. He viewed these contemporary issues in light of traditional chauvinist foundations of Chinese society. "China had polygamy in the early 1900s. That's two generations separated from polygamy," he explained. "I have friends whose grandfathers had multiple wives. So the culture of monogamy is not as set. It might just be the people I hang out with, but a lot of them don't think twice about cheating on a girlfriend."

Similarly, David's own family history led him to believe that current practices of cheating and having mistresses are still an important marker of male status in China. "There's this idea that the more successful a man is, it's almost accepted as part of the status that he would have a mistress," he explained. "[In] my father's generation, there were like thirteen brothers and sisters, but that's all from the second wife, right? So there's just this idea of 'if I'm able to support more than one woman, then I'll do that.'" Although David preferred to be monogamous with his partner, he nonetheless accepted that male cheating is "part of the structure" of Chinese society.

STIGMATIZED FEMININITIES: ABC WOMEN'S DOWNWARD SEXUAL MOBILITY

Ultimately, whether or not men used cultural in-betweenness to their advantage with local women, it is undeniably clear that this was *their* choice to make. Compared to the United States, they were greatly empowered in their romantic options in the ethnic homeland. By contrast, Chinese American women's education, skills, and independent mindsets—qualities that propelled their careers forward—led to a drastic plunge in their romantic desirability in the PRC. Their so-called downward sexual mobility is comparable to that experienced by white expat women in East Asia, who face social isolation and limited dating opportunities in Japan, Taiwan, and China.[50] In fact, "China is often described as sexual purgatory for Western women."[51] A study based in Shanghai argues that their lack of dating options stems from several areas: an unwillingness to date local men, the belief that local men are not attracted to foreign women, and their certainty that "Western men can get a Chinese woman easier than a Western one and often a younger and sexier one at that."[52] Still, this trend is especially striking in light of heterosexual white women's privileged social status in their home countries, which provides plentiful dating options if they so desire.

Female ABCs who wanted a relationship also found themselves competing against a vast pool of attractive young local women for a small number of foreign guys. For the most part, these women were not interested in dating locals; they perceived Chinese men as having traditional expectations of relationships—including women having more economic and emotional dependence and bearing the brunt of housework and childcare responsibilities. Joy, an attractive executive who looked far younger than her thirty-four years, gave an example: "If I dated a local guy I might ask him, 'Do you expect me to cook? Do you expect me to stay home after I give birth to raise the children?' I think there's more expectations on that side. 'Do you respect my individuality? Can I make decisions myself without consulting you?'" In her view, Chinese men "probably want the woman to be less direct and more feminine" as opposed to traits she placed in high regard, such as "always speaking your mind and having a very strong will."

Highly educated ABC women who moved abroad for career purposes prided themselves on their financial and social independence, proactivity, and decision-making. Celebrated as sources of female empowerment in the United States, a context in which not getting married is an increasingly acceptable life option, these qualities are largely stigmatized for Chinese women.[53] Consequently, female ancestral homeland migrants had difficulty finding the types of relationships they would seek back home: namely, egalitarian partnerships with men of similar educational attainment, life experience, and outlook. Thirty-four-year-old corporate manager Cindy, who had recently separated from her ABC husband, gave a common perspective: "I can't see myself dating a local. I would want to date someone who has more exposure outside of China. I would want him to be more well-rounded and have similar experience and background as myself." She added, "But I don't think that [ABC] guys really care about that as much as women do."

For Chinese American women who *were* interested in dating native Chinese men, structural and gendered power differences posed obstacles to the couple's future together—issues that would generally not cause major problems if the genders were reversed. Kelly explained, "Even if you found someone who was *willing* to date a local guy, the number of local Chinese men who are willing to date a Chinese American woman is *much* lower than the amount of local women who are dying to marry a Chinese American man." She raised certain other key points: "If the [men] want to stay [in China], can they keep their Chinese American wife here? [Plus,] you probably make more money than your local Chinese counterpart, and that's also kind of a big deal. I would say most men here are not comfortable with that."

Many male participants acknowledged that local norms heavily limited the options of their female ABC friends. Paul believed that "Chinese American women have a very difficult time here." Like George, he was deeply critical of Chinese gender relations, tracing them back to the nation's history of male chauvinism. "I think a lot of it is because [in] relationship matters, Chinese men like weak women. They like docile women," he noted critically. "The roots of where women come from is, basically they're inside the house, you know? And so I think Chinese American women have a particularly hard time because no Chinese men really want to date them because they're not that. They speak their minds and they don't give *mianzi* [face], right? And they appear more affluent and sociable and more cosmopolitan than them."

Women's egalitarian expectations served as barriers to finding stable partnerships in local expatriate communities. Furthermore, the temporary nature of expat life encouraged a more casual approach to dating. Thirty-three-year-old Michelle, who married a British man she met in Beijing, described their relationship as "almost a miracle" because "no one thinks long-term [and] everyone is just out to have fun. So as a result, it's not really conducive for long-term relationships."

Along these lines, I talked to Joanne, a thirty-one-year-old financial consultant who had been living in China for six years. Uninterested in dating locals, she had engaged in three different relationships of one-and-a-half to two years apiece with different expat men. All ended because China "is a very transitory place, and each of these guys were like, 'Well, my time in Shanghai is done.'" One moved back to Italy, another to Spain, and the third relocated to Singapore. Joanne was working between eighty and a hundred hours per week for a multinational firm and had not considered any of the relationships serious enough to move with her boyfriends, who understood that she was prioritizing her career. "They knew me well enough that there wasn't even a question" of moving with them, she explained. "It wasn't even like, 'Oh, you could go work in Europe,' because I'd be like, 'No' . . . the answer was known before it was even asked."

For their part, expat men often viewed relationships with Western women as requiring more work and consideration, whereas they treated local women as temporary, casual flings. George acknowledged that ABC women had higher standards and expectations than native Chinese. "I think for a lot of expats, dating a Chinese American girl is like a real relationship, whereas dating a Chinese girl is just sort of sampling a foreign culture." Despite being seriously involved with a local woman with whom he was discussing marriage, George still felt that "there's a lot more commitment [to] dating a Chinese American girl than there is to dating a Chinese girl."

Similar to Lee's findings in South Korea,[54] it was common for female ABCs in this study to create social distance from local women as a way of constructing themselves as more culturally advanced and empowered. ABC women tended to view native Chinese women in their age range in two stereotypical ways: either as nightclubbing gold diggers who lacked manners, education, and self-respect, or as traditional-minded, naive dependents who married the first guy they dated. Twenty-five-year-old Natalie thought ABC women might actually be more popular among expat men because of these stereotypes. "As an Asian American girl, you're almost more valued because you're not gonna squat down in the middle of the street. You're not gonna expect somebody to get married just because you slept together," she commented snidely. "You're a little less high maintenance in some ways, and they can bring you to their functions, whereas maybe they might be a little embarrassed to bring someone who's really pretty [but] couldn't interact with their colleagues."

While many expressed reservations about dating locals, it is important to note that three ABC women I interviewed were either married to or in serious committed relationships with native Chinese men. For example, thirty-three-year-old Ellen was introduced to her husband Jimmy five years earlier by a mutual friend. She recalled her skepticism at the time: "When my friend was setting me up, I was not interested. 'I don't see how it would ever work out—I'm not interested in meeting a Chinese guy.'" Jimmy, however, had developed an extremely global outlook through study abroad in New Zealand and two decades of English training. Eventually he opened a travel company that brought him into daily contact with Westerners. Ellen observed certain key differences between herself and her husband but was unsure as to whether they were based on culture, gender, or both. "We had very different childhoods. Very different background of families, but I feel like it's always hard to know where it is culture versus personality," she reflected. "Sometimes I feel like, 'Oh, you know, he's not as emotionally communicative.' But like, how many guys are? I mean, 'cause he's Chinese? Or is it 'cause he's a guy? Or is it 'cause he's a Chinese guy?" Ellen cocked her head to the side and thought for a moment. "I don't know," she sighed.

Still, these individuals were the exception. Most ABC women were not very open to dating locals and thus faced far more challenges in creating fulfilling personal lives than did men. This situation caused single women to confront a difficult set of decisions that pitted their careers against finding a romantic relationship.

White Western women in China take various approaches to their romantic marginalization, including emotional resignation, resistance, increased sexual aggressiveness, sometimes dating local men, and geographic mobility—as in, moving away.[55] Regarding this last strategy, a survey of Western women professionals in Japan found a similar phenomenon. For a large proportion of the single women surveyed, which included a number of high-level executives, "the primary reason they will not extend their stay in Japan is the limited dating opportunities."[56] This situation conflicted with the high levels of excitement, pride, and confidence they tended to express about their work accomplishments.

Correspondingly, single ABC women I spoke with admitted facing a difficult decision: should they disrupt their careers to move to areas with more dating possibilities? Amy, a twenty-six-year-old social entrepreneur, remarked that regardless of a Chinese American man's experience in the United States, "they come here, and they become douchebags because they're so sought after." She believed that this was the reason why "there aren't that many women compared to men here who stay for longer than five years, because we really do have different considerations." Amy noted sadly that many of her girlfriends had moved away after being unable to find a partner in China. Similarly, Benjamin observed that while many of his female friends in Shanghai had great careers there and wanted to stay, "they all end up leaving because they want to get married, they want to meet a stable boyfriend, they want to have a husband. It's too tough here."

Thirty-two-year-old tech manager Sophia was at such a transition point when we met. After earning her MBA from a top American business school, she had spent three years working at start-up companies in Shanghai and was considering leaving her current position. Rather than seek another job there, Sophia was contemplating returning to the United States to find a relationship. Gloomily, she reasoned, "If I was five years younger, I would say I'm going to stay in China and try to find something new, but now

I'm thirty-two. I'm going to be thirty-three soon. I'm single and very single. It's not like I want to have babies right now or that I'm feeling really sad and lonely because I need a boyfriend [but] I'm going to have less options as I get older. I should really probably do something about this. It's more like a rational thing, and I hate that I have to think about it." Within six months of our conversation, Sophia had relocated to San Francisco. Although I was not able to follow up with her, undoubtedly her chances of finding a relationship there were far higher than they had been in Shanghai.

Other single ABC women stayed in China for their careers, knowing that their odds of locating a partner were slim. Joy described finding a relationship as "impossible." She stated, somewhat defiantly, "It's difficult because we always compete for the expat men who are getting a lot of attention and flattery from the local girls. Being expat women, you're like, 'I'm not going to sacrifice anything for you. I do fine myself. I can support myself. . . . Why do I need you? Why should I sacrifice for you?'" Like many others, she set herself apart from local women with her remark: "I think local girls have much more to gain financially if they date an expat man."

However, when I asked whether she would consider moving back to the United States for the sake of her personal life, Joy explained that her career was flourishing in Shanghai and she wasn't sure she could take the risk. "I've been out of the [U.S. job] market for ten years and don't know what kind of job I can find. Can I get a six-figure job? Then, if not, what am I sacrificing?" Joy was also doubtful about the certainty of securing a relationship in the United States, wryly noting that many of her career-minded female friends in New York were "not finding anyone" either.

Conclusion

This chapter has shown how gender figures centrally in the lives of ancestral homeland migrants. They are elite members of the "transnational capitalist class,"[57] serving as cultural and economic bridges between global superpowers, yet these same Chinese

Americans are differently affected by local constructions of femininity and masculinity. Understanding how gender shapes ABCs' trajectories and decision-making brings more complexity to our understanding of how and why people move between countries and cultures. This process requires people to negotiate new norms and reconfigure their personal identities while abroad. Consequently, my sample includes more Chinese American men who were seriously dating, engaged to, or married to local women, whereas ABC women who arrived single were also much more likely to stay that way. In 2018, I conducted follow-up interviews with five men who still lived in China and found that the two individuals who were single when we first spoke had both married local women.

Gender shapes ancestral homeland migration by expanding social options for men while contracting those for women. Although members of both genders enjoyed professional opportunities and rapid career progression, local patriarchal structures provided heterosexual men with a dizzying array of romantic options and a much-resuscitated sense of racialized masculinity. ABC women, who are constructed as highly desirable (albeit in deeply problematic ways) back home, find their options severely constrained in the PRC. There are limited options to deal with this type of social marginalization: they may leave China or choose to stay, with no guarantee of a relationship if they so desire. Heterosexual single professional women thus must choose between their careers or their personal lives, while their male counterparts can enjoy both. The significance of expatriates to the global economy might mean that women's limited relationship prospects could actually impede their ability to exert influence on key aspects of international business and decision-making. Hence, because migrants are "socially and spatially situated subjects" occupying "classed, gendered and racialized bodies" in particular nationalist projects, state formations and border crossings,"[58] it is integral to factor in gender to fully understand ancestral homeland migration to China.

6

Conclusion

This book has sought to understand what it means to be Chinese American in an increasingly transnational age. Global capitalism has played a central role in the relocation of upper-middle-class second-generation ABCs to their ethnic homeland. As these pages have illustrated, these highly educated professionals were primarily drawn to China for economic reasons, which distinguishes them from groups of return migrants whose travels are inspired by cultural connection. Although my participants could likely have attained a very comfortable standard of living without ever leaving home, the social and cultural capital they brought with them from the United States, in combination with their shared ethnic ancestry, opened the door for numerous career opportunities and rapid advancement in their ancestral homeland. For the past two decades, these workers have quietly forged socioeconomic ties between the world's two most powerful nations, even as U.S.-China relations have become progressively adversarial.

This analysis has also explored how the personal identities of ABCs are altered, challenged, or reinforced through their long-term immersion in Chinese society. On the surface, moving away from the United States, where they are viewed as perpetually foreign, to the PRC, where they are considered perpetually Chinese, seems as if it would guarantee a deeper sense of racial, ethnic, and cultural belonging. Indeed, many of my respondents greatly enjoyed the sense of freedom and anonymity of fitting in with the ethnic majority. Nevertheless, I have shown how residing in the ancestral homeland does not automatically generate feelings of belonging. This is because, regardless of whether they are in the United States or in China, ABCs are slotted into rigid, oppositional categories that seek to differentiate Chinese from Americans, foreigners from natives, and non-Westerners from Westerners. Binary classifications such as these disregard the rich, nuanced, and fundamentally hybrid nature of their lived experiences.

Rather than be constrained by these narrow categorizations, my participants found novel ways to capitalize on the assumptions that others made about them to boost opportunities for personal advancement in China. Depending on the context and desired outcome, ABCs knowingly leveraged their social ambiguity with mainlanders and non-Chinese Westerners alike, shifting like chameleons between different ethnic options. As they alternated between American, Chinese American, Chinese, or Taiwanese presentations of self, the ability to convincingly perform flexible ethnicity for different audiences was key to their overall success.

How these elite migrants deployed strategic in-betweenness to navigate the norms of their parental homeland illustrates the fluidity of racial-ethnic identity and cultural belonging within transnational spaces. The construction of identity is an ongoing, iterative process formed through the interactions between individuals and the larger social context, which is itself constantly shifting. Therefore, the identities of diasporic Chinese are continually evolving in relationship to the PRC's domestic and global transformations. Despite the common Western tendency to essentialize China as an ancient monolithic culture, Tu Weiming reminds us that it "has never been a static structure but [is instead] a dynamic, constantly changing landscape."[1]

For my respondents, being primordially linked to China and Chinese culture allowed them to effectively use strategic in-betweenness even though they did not fully comprehend every social nuance. At the same time, their social ambiguity caused local people to hold them to far higher standards of language ability and cultural competence as compared to their non-Chinese colleagues. Thus, ABCs generally gained the most by staying within a limited range of positions where they could serve as cultural liaisons between the United States and China—especially as representatives of multinational companies or as self-employed entrepreneurs introducing Western concepts and products to the PRC's exploding population of middle-class consumers.

Nevertheless, over the years in which I conducted this research, it became evident that the professional opportunities for ABCs and other white-collar expatriate workers were narrowing significantly within China's global cities. Positions once easily obtained by Westerners were increasingly being filled by highly skilled, overseas-educated *haigui*. This trend has pushed many ABCs out of the local market as well as prompted those who remain to continually strive to enhance their skill sets to remain competitive within the country's now much more developed economy. The era of seemingly limitless opportunity and expansion that characterized the 1990s and early 2000s—referred to colloquially as the "wild, wild West"—has effectively drawn to a close. Many respondents predicted that they and other Western professionals would likely only enjoy another five to ten years of comparative advantage.

For most individuals, moving to the PRC did not represent a "return" to a longed-for emotional homeland. At the same time, I have argued for the importance of taking life-course stage into account. When ancestral homeland migration is viewed as a circular process, it is possible to see how these journeys might be prompted by certain phases of an individual's life. Hence, even though the ABCs I met sought to build careers in China during their late twenties and early thirties, many had already spent extended periods of time there as teenagers and young adults. Similar to other roots tourists, during earlier homeland trips they sought to build cultural connection with the country by learning Mandarin, visiting ancestral villages, and bonding with extended family members. These types of early transnational experiences were able to help some younger adults resolve identity-based issues that emerged from growing up as racialized minorities in the United States.

Finally, this book has used an intersectional lens to analyze the impact of gender—along with social class, race-ethnicity, and nationality—on the social lives and trajectories of ABCs in Beijing and Shanghai. Although members of both genders achieved comparable amounts of professional success, which suggests the existence of less of a glass ceiling/bamboo ceiling effect in China compared to the United States, local patriarchal norms allowed heterosexual men to profit more from their elevated global status in terms of both dating and establishing long-term, committed relationships. ABC men who have long been subject to emasculating racialized stereotypes in the United States experienced vastly expanded romantic options in the ancestral homeland. By contrast, their female counterparts found that their ages, educational qualifications, independent mindsets, and desire for egalitarian partnerships led to diminished prospects. Consequently, local gender norms enhanced men's ability to realize both satisfying careers and personal lives overseas, whereas women were more likely to be forced to prioritize one or the other. This form of social inequality is easily overlooked when attention is paid solely to the professional realm.

Should I Stay or Should I Go? Deciding to Leave the Ancestral Homeland

In 2020, I was able to locate forty-five of my respondents, who, in the intervening years, had scattered across the world. The majority had departed the PRC, with twenty-two returning to the United States and five relocating to Australia, Kenya, Switzerland, and Taiwan. On the whole, returnees to the United States were doing extremely well in their careers and had found ways to transfer the skills they gained in China to an American context. A large proportion were employed as directors or high-level managers for information technology companies and multinational corporations that interfaced with the Pacific Rim.

Eighteen people still remained in China, although only a select few planned to stay there indefinitely. Aside from the changing economic landscape, individuals most often cited quality of life concerns—particularly the environmental pollution and limited educational options for children—as the main factors pushing them out of the country. In line with broader patterns of circular migration, the choice to leave the ancestral homeland generally coincided with the next life-course stage of marriage and child-rearing.

Jenny, who had a very successful marketing career as well as close relatives in Beijing, explained why she eventually wanted to raise her children in the more comfortable context of the United States: "I don't think I can raise kids here. It's just so hard. It's expensive. The air is polluted. Everything is not safe. And I see, even though my own family here is doing very well economically, the amount of pain and trouble that [people] have to go through in order to be able to ensure that their kids have the best of stuff. I'm just like, 'No, I'm going to go back to the U.S., move to a relatively good neighborhood, and send my kids to a public school.' It just seems like it's way too much competition here to be able to raise a kid properly."

Nonetheless, the global, cosmopolitan outlook cultivated by ABCs over their years abroad led many to remain open about the possibility of moving back to the PRC—or at least to East Asia—should the right opportunity arise. For instance, after working in Beijing for half a decade, Lee and his wife decided to leave for the sake of their young child. He clarified, however, that their departure was not necessarily permanent: "I don't think this is just this phase in my life where I came here and got involved with China, and then I'll leave it behind and go on to other things. . . . But I would like to take a break from it, after living here for five years straight. Plus, I have a very young daughter now. I'm more worried about the environment and the pollution, and I feel like, when she's at a very young age and physically developing, it's better to live in a cleaner environment, so I'll . . . reengage with China again at a later stage."

Furthermore, even when planning a return home, most participants sought to continue engaging with the country in a more limited form. Jonathan provided a typical response when asked how long he planned to stay in Shanghai: "[I'll be here] at least another three to five years. Whatever I do after this I think will be related to China. Ideally I'd be able to work in the States full-time but have a job that requires me to come out several times a year or to live out here for a certain segment of the year." Perceiving American suburban life as mundane, he sought to remain connected to China's dynamism. "I love America and eventually I want to be back there someday, but what you realize is, life back there would feel so narrow," he remarked. "Because here, you constantly interact with interesting people that are coming from all over the place. But I could just imagine if I move back to LA, to some suburb somewhere, it's static. I think I'd be totally bored!"

Like those who had left, the individuals who remained in the ancestral homeland had continued to achieve notable career success as they further leveraged their in-betweenness and widened their skill sets and social networks. In the intervening years, nearly all had changed positions or moved to different companies, which usually involved promotions to higher levels of authority. Their priorities, nonetheless, had also begun to shift as they entered the next stage of life. Take the example of forty-year-old Benjamin, a Shanghai-based entrepreneur. When we first spoke in 2013, he and his wife were busy running their own businesses and did not yet have children. In the years since, he had sold his company, earned an EMBA, and helped to build a large, extremely lucrative start-up in China while also raising a young daughter and son. Having realized his financial goals, Benjamin was taking a self-imposed break from work to contemplate his next steps and reflect on his legacy. "I'm forty years old. I have a family to take care of. . . . I'm looking at my own life and what I want to accomplish, what I want to become. *It's not just about the money,*" he stated introspectively. "How do I want to be remembered when I'm sixty, sixty-five, and retiring? . . . So, I'm deep in thought these days."

From Invisibility to Hypervisibility: Being Chinese American during a Global Pandemic

Initially, I had planned to use these final pages to suggest, with tempered optimism, that the United States has become far more welcoming of Chinese Americans than when my respondents were growing up. To be sure, recent years have seen a remarkable surge of mainstream films and television shows that portray Asians and Asian Americans in complex, three-dimensional ways. The South Korean film *Parasite* swept the 2020 Academy Awards and was the first non-English language film in Oscar history to win the award for Best Picture. Furthermore, many of this book's themes were brought to life on-screen in the films *Crazy Rich Asians* (2018) and *The Farewell* (2019), introducing mostly white mainstream audiences to the struggles of ABCs who reconcile their sense of in-betweenness by engaging with China and Chinese culture.

Tragically, since I first began writing this chapter, the world has radically transformed due to the novel coronavirus that first originated in Wuhan, China, at the end of 2019. In the space of only a few short months, COVID-19 has upended the daily lives of billions of people across the globe and wreaked catastrophic, long-lasting economic damage. In the United States, this pandemic has also exposed the tenuous nature of genuine cultural acceptance of Asians and Asian Americans. Seemingly overnight, the "positive" stereotype of Asian model minorities has reverted back to ugly representations of Asians as a threatening, disease-bearing "yellow peril": the same racist discourse that was used to justify the Chinese Exclusion Act of 1882.

In an era of emboldened white supremacy and xenophobia stoked by President Trump, who referred to COVID-19 as the "Chinese virus" in early press conferences at least twenty separate times,[2] a steady onslaught of virulent racism has been unleashed on those assumed to be Chinese. An online reporting center for bias incidents against Asian Americans (launched in March 2020) received, at its height, up to one hundred reports per day.[3] Across the United States and a range of other Western countries, Asian people have been verbally harassed, spat on, and even physically attacked by strangers. In a horrific incident at a wholesale Sam's Club in Texas, a Burmese American father and his two young children (ages two and six) were brutally stabbed by a young man in an attack the FBI labeled a hate crime. After being apprehended, the perpetrator told police he intended to kill them "because he thought the family was Chinese and infecting people with the coronavirus."[4]

In an eloquent op-ed article in the *New York Times*, poet Cathy Park Hong describes the disconcerting feelings of pain and fear gripping Asian Americans who have long been taught to downplay their own racial marginalization:

> In the past, I had a habit of minimizing anti-Asian racism because it had been drilled into me early on that racism against Asians didn't exist. Anytime that I raised concerns about a racial comment, I was told that it wasn't racial. Anytime I brought up an anti-Asian incident, a white person interjected that it was a distraction from the more important issue (and there was always a more important issue). I've been conditioned to think my second-class citizenry was low on the scale of oppression and therefore not worth bringing up even though every single Asian-American I know has stories of being emasculated, fetishized, humiliated, underpaid, fired or demoted because of our racial identities.[5]

This hateful violence has emerged from a flawed logic that conflates Chinese Americans with China itself. In many ways, this broad distrust of Asians in the United States harks back to the infamous case against Wen Ho Lee, the Taiwanese American scientist who was accused, and then acquitted, of stealing U.S. state secrets for the PRC in the late 1990s. Reflecting on the unjust legacies of the case two decades later, journalist Lowen Liu writes that Lee's predicament "taught Chinese Americans that their country may never trust them" and that they "ultimately do not have a say over their own Americanness."[6] In other words, the belonging of

ABCs in the United States is entirely conditional on the whims of mainstream white society.

Being targets of harassment and violence based on perceived racial and cultural differences is not only frightening but also unfamiliar for many middle-class ABCs such as myself, who have grown up cushioned by the model minority myth. My hope is that despite the intense anguish, confusion, and isolation provoked by the racialized othering of Chinese/Asian Americans, stronger social and political alliances will be forged with other marginalized groups of color—particularly African Americans— that have long been forced to endure such treatment. As Kelsey Liu and Monica Hahn write, "Asians can and should take time to grieve and process the trauma of what we're experiencing. But it's also time to push our collective racial consciousness forward, past insular self-awareness and toward cross-racial solidarity. We need to contextualize this current moment as part of the larger story of American racial oppression."[7]

The Fading American Dream and the Rising Chinese Dream

On the global level, U.S.-China relations have quickly devolved from tense to disastrous. The American and Chinese regimes have engaged in a blame-filled war of words about the origins and development of the COVID-19 crisis, accelerating existing acrimony from the protracted trade war instigated by President Trump in 2018 (an initiative experts roundly faulted as ineffective and, before the pandemic, "one of the biggest threats to the global economy").[8] Experts have even begun to fear the onset of a new Cold War.

Public opinion in both countries has mirrored these negative trends. A Pew Research Center poll of Americans from April 2020 found that 66 percent held a negative view of China—a drop of 20 percent from the beginning of the Trump administration.[9] Meanwhile, admiration of the United States has plummeted in equal measure in the PRC as citizens grow more suspicious of the American government and political system. Another survey, also from April 2020, found that only 39 percent of Chinese people held a favorable view of the United States, compared to 58 percent just one year earlier.[10] Indeed, "once starry-eyed enthusiasm for America among many Chinese has given way to sober admiration, if not outright disillusionment, as people have gotten to know the United States better and its problems have come into clearer view."[11]

Charles, who worked in Shanghai for four years, followed by stints in the United Kingdom, Hong Kong, and San Francisco, offered a cogent analysis of the current global situation: "China has definitely earned its stripes as a world power, and naturally there will be friction between a rising power and a superpower. The Trump administration's insistence on a trade war really brought that to the forefront, and I fear that it will only get worse as time goes on. China is being cast as 'the enemy' or 'the Other,' and it will negatively affect Chinese Americans in the U.S. The pandemic has laid bare how interconnected the two countries are. . . . Both need each other, but both don't like and [also] mistrust each other."

This situation has unfolded against a backdrop of intensified Chinese nationalism that has accompanied the country's massive expansion of international influence across the African continent and other parts of the developing world in particular. Once-positive rhetoric about the American Dream in China has been replaced by that of the Chinese dream (*zhongguo meng*), a concept first popularized by President Xi Jinping in 2012. This slogan has been used to inspire a renewed patriotism in young people, encouraging them to work toward collective goals of "a prosperous country, national revival, and people's well-being."[12] Symbolizing the government's long-term vision of the future, the Chinese dream is broken into detailed five-year plans that establish the PRC as a true world leader instead of a developing nation.

My respondents who remained in China had observed this increase in national fervor. Alan, who first moved to Shanghai in 2010 and was still living there a decade later, noted a palpable shift in local mentality from a focus on individual profit to one of collective pride. As evidence, he raised the example of the action film *Wolf Warrior 2* (2017). The highest-grossing Chinese motion picture of all time, the plot centers around a PRC soldier who single-handedly saves an unspecified African country from destruction. In one provocative poster, the hero stands with his middle finger extended defiantly toward the camera. A patch on his arm declares in English, "I fight for China," while underneath, a large tagline of dark red Chinese characters reads, "Anyone who offends China, no matter how remote, must be exterminated."[13]

Journalist Helen Raleigh warns against dismissing this action movie as pure entertainment. Instead, it represents a global changing of the guard. The film "clearly presents what China's rise means to China: The country's inevitable rise to world-power status corresponds to the inevitable decline of the old world power, the U.S.," she writes. "China is not only destined for greatness but also responsible for replacing the old world order with a new one led by China—one where the U.S. is not only a loser but practically irrelevant."[14] Similarly, Alan viewed the film through the lens of growing American isolationism under the Trump administration. "America has been pushed to the outside," he stated, his voice tinged with disappointment. "It's like the whole world . . . has teamed up, and the U.S. is just really on its own, with its own agenda."

The Uncertain Future of Chinese American Ancestral Homeland Migration

Back in 2014, I interviewed an entrepreneur named Eric in Beijing. After four years there, the talkative twenty-eight-year-old had achieved a far higher pay grade than his peers back home and had no plans to leave, despite being very critical of the local quality of life. When asked whether he had moved to China in search of the American Dream, Eric fervently disagreed. He drew a stark contrast between his immigrant parents' more holistic motivations for migrating to the United States long ago with his own self-serving reasons for working in the ancestral homeland:

> I think the American Dream was that [my parents] wanted to go to the States, wanted to have much better living standards, [a] much better medical system, much better schools. . . . In

general, you have a better future and better outlook. All these Asian parents worked so hard just to have their kids be born in the States and receive better education, be more worldly-minded than others that are stuck or left behind. [For me,] coming here wasn't for that. *It was just for the money, for the continuation of the career.* . . . Coming here is more for the financial part, as opposed to the American Dream. Because the American Dream is insurance. [There's a] financial part as well, but it's for that quality of life. Because everyone who lives in Beijing complains about Beijing all the time. I'm one of them. . . . I do not like this place. But, it's for the market.

The self-assurance—what some might even call arrogance—with which Eric spoke was the result of having a clear comparative advantage in the Chinese economy. As we have seen, however, within the space of a few short years, the country's global ascendance has definitively curtailed professional possibilities for second-generation ABCs. In the process, their ability to leverage strategic in-betweenness has become less effective in China's global cities. Due to this quickly transforming social and economic landscape, the analysis presented in this book only captures a finite snapshot in time.

So, what does all of this mean for Chinese American ancestral homeland migration? Once predictable patterns have been destabilized by the as-yet-to-be-determined consequences of the COVID-19 crisis, especially in terms of the PRC's heavily tarnished international image and the ongoing global economic downturn. Ultimately, it remains to be seen whether this form of migration will be considered a short-lived, historically contingent trend produced by China's economic boom or whether ABC professionals will continue to move there in large numbers. As financial prospects begin to fade, homeland travel may become more motivated by cultural connection with the country. In the midst of an unclear future, this book constitutes just the first step toward understanding the experiences of these transnational Chinese Americans whose lives straddle the borders of belonging.

Appendix
Research Methods

This study is based on semistructured in-depth interviews with sixty self-identified American-born Chinese individuals (half women, half men) who were living and working in the People's Republic of China. The interviews took place during the summers of 2013, 2014, and 2018 in the cities of Beijing and Shanghai. In 2013, I conducted thirty-three interviews; in 2014, I conducted nineteen interviews; and in 2018, I conducted eight new interviews, in addition to eight in-depth follow-up interviews with respondents from prior years. In order to qualify for the study, individuals had to self-identify as an ABC and had to have lived and worked in either Beijing or Shanghai for a minimum of one year. Several had only been there for six months, but I included their perspectives because they had all lived in China previously in their lives.

In 2013 and 2014, I recruited respondents through personal contacts and through Listserv electronic mailing lists of American universities and professional organizations in Beijing and Shanghai; in 2018, I largely recruited new participants using WeChat (China's predominant social media and messaging mobile application). Participants also referred me to their Chinese American friends and colleagues, which allowed me to expand the respondent group through snowball sampling. The interviews, which lasted between one and three hours, took place at participants' homes or in public establishments, such as restaurants or coffee shops. Twelve took place over Skype or WeChat.

TABLE A.1. Demographic Characteristics of Sample

		FREQUENCY	PERCENTAGE*
Gender	Female	30	50%
	Male	30	50%
Place of birth	USA	44	73%
	China	8	13%
	Taiwan	7	12%
	Brazil	1	2%
Education	BA	31	52%
	MA	15	25%
	MBA	6	10%
	Law degree	4	7%
	PhD	3	5%
	No college	1	2%
Age	22–24	5	8%
	25–29	19	32%
	30–39	30	50%
	40–46	6	10%
	Mean = 32		
Time in China	Mean = 4.8 years		
Profession	Entrepreneur	10	17%
	Corporate sales	8	13%
	Education	8	13%
	Finance	7	12%
	Creative/arts	7	12%
	Marketing/PR	5	8%
	Health care	4	7%
	Tech/IT	4	7%
	Law	3	5%
	Journalism	3	5%
	Other	1	2%

* Some percentages add up to 101 due to rounding.

All interviews were semistructured, beginning with a common list of questions that were flexible enough to pursue individualized topics. Questions were organized into the thematic areas of childhood and cultural identity; motivations for moving to China; experiences of living and working in China as a Chinese American; and gender-based issues. Due to my focus on gender, I purposely sought to have an equal number of female and male participants. My own position as a second-generation ABC who had lived in China for nearly three years, and therefore had a shared bicultural background and experience with the ancestral homeland, assisted me in recruiting respondents as well as establishing rapport with them during interviews.

With participants' consent, the interviews were recorded and transcribed. I coded the transcripts using the qualitative data analysis software NVivo and employed grounded theory to develop a detailed coding system and to generate broader theoretical themes.[1] I conducted an initial coding of the first set of interviews, and by simultaneously collecting and analyzing data over an extended period, I was able to follow up on these analytical insights in subsequent interviews to clarify emergent concepts—particularly that of strategic in-betweenness.[2]

Acknowledgments

From its inception, this project has been a labor of love. My interest in Chinese American professionals who have "returned" to live and work in their ancestral homeland began after I read an article on this topic in the *New York Times* in 2013. As a second-generation ABC who studied abroad in Beijing during college and then later returned for professional reasons, this subject resonated with me on a uniquely personal level. I began conducting interviews for *Chasing the American Dream in China* while still in the midst of wrapping up fieldwork for my first book, which examined a very different set of issues. Little could I imagine at the time that my curiosity would eventually lead to the publication of another book.

Undoubtedly this project would not have become a book at all if not for the support of Rutgers University Press. Thank you to editor Lisa Banning, who reached out to me at the Association for Asian American Studies annual meeting in 2017 and first proposed the idea. I am deeply grateful for Lisa's enthusiastic support, guidance, and encouragement throughout this process. This book also benefited immensely from the efforts of editor Jasper Chang, who took over managing Rutgers's Asian American Studies Today series from Lisa with grace and professionalism.

My ideas have been enhanced and furthered by my incomparable colleagues. First and foremost, I am grateful to Sonali Jain, Helene Lee, Mytoan Nguyen-Akbar, and Jane Yamashiro—experts on ancestral homeland migration to Asia, who generously offered their feedback on my project during numerous conferences and personal conversations. Thanks goes to Andrea Louie and Lisong Li, who, along with Helene and Jane, read my full manuscript and provided invaluable critiques during a daylong book workshop. I also received useful feedback on several chapters from my colleagues at UMass Boston, including Sofya Aptekar, Andrea Leverentz, Sarah Mayorga-Gallo, and Jason Rodriquez. Finally, Jenny Gavacs's superb developmental editing helped to tie the analysis together, and Letta Page greatly improved the prose.

Financial support for research, writing, and travel to China was made possible by grants from the University of Massachusetts Boston. Over the years, I learned a great deal from the insights of audiences at the Graduate School of Education and the International Migration Working Group at Harvard University, SUNY Albany, Beijing Normal University, the University of California Irvine, and Université Sorbonne Nouvelle. I also presented portions of this work at the annual meetings of the American Sociological Association, the Association for Asian Studies, the Association for Asian American Studies, and the Eastern Sociological Society.

Earlier versions of parts of this book have appeared previously in "'Leftover Women' and 'Kings of the Candy Shop': Gendering Chinese American Ancestral Homeland Migration to China," *American Behavioral Scientist* 61, no. 10 (2017): 1172–1191; and "The Benefits of In-Betweenness: Return Migration of Second-Generation Chinese American Professionals to China," *Journal of Ethnic and Migration Studies* 42, no. 12 (2016): 1941–1958. Thank you to the publishers for their permission to use these materials.

Finally, I am forever indebted to my family and friends for their unconditional love and support as I have followed my dreams across the country and around the world. I extend the deepest gratitude to my parents, Kim and Harry, and to my siblings, Elaine and Steve, for their continual encouragement. Over the course of completing this manuscript, my life has completely transformed in the best of ways. This book is thus dedicated to my incredible partner, Dino, and our beautiful son, Theo. You both inspire me to become a little bit better every day.

Notes

Chapter 1   Introduction

1. To protect the identity of individuals, all proper names have been given pseudonyms unless otherwise specified.

2. South Koreans constitute the most populous foreign group in China. Korean students also make up the largest number of study abroad students in the country, numbering over seventy thousand in 2016. Marsh 2017.

3. "Second generation" refers to U.S.-born offspring of at least one foreign-born parent from China, Hong Kong, or Taiwan. I am also including those who were born abroad but arrived in the United States with their parents before age twelve. For a definition, see Portes and Zhou 2012.

4. Pew Research Center Social and Demographic Trends 2017.

5. Wike and Devlin 2018.

6. Kibria 2000, 78.

7. Dikötter 2015.

8. Trading Economics, n.d.

9. Schmitz 2017.

10. Ambler 2017.

11. Hernandez and Bui 2018. It is important to note that much of this economic growth has stalled since the onset of the COVID-19 pandemic that began in early 2020. I take note of these changes in the book's conclusion.

12. Kawai 2005, 112.

13. The U.S. Census Bureau defines an "Asian" individual as "a person having origins in any of the original peoples of the Far East, Southeast

Asia, or the Indian subcontinent including, for example, Cambodia, China, India, Japan, Korea, Malaysia, Pakistan, the Philippine Islands, Thailand, and Vietnam." U.S. Census Bureau 2019.

14. Echeverria-Estrada and Batalova 2020.
15. National Bureau of Statistics of China 2011.
16. Fechter 2016, 22.
17. H. K. Lee 2018, 5.
18. Yoo, Burrola, and Steger 2010, 115.
19. Yoo, Burrola, and Steger 2010, 115.
20. See Kawai 2005; Chou and Feagin 2015.
21. Kochhar and Cilluffo 2018.
22. Yam 2017.
23. Yoo, Burrola, and Steger 2010.
24. Lin et al. 2005.
25. A. Louie 2004, 12.
26. Tuan 1998.
27. L. L. Wang 1991, 182.
28. L. L. Wang 1991, 182.
29. Nagel 1994, 154.
30. K. B. Chan 2005, 17.
31. L. K. Wang 2016, 1941.
32. Tuan 1998.
33. Ong 1999.
34. See Waters 1990; Vasquez 2010.
35. Purkayastha 2005, 5.
36. See Waldinger 2015; Foner 2005; Basch, Schiller, and Blanc 1994.
37. Schiller, Basch, and Blanc-Szanton 1992, 1.
38. Ley and Kobayashi 2005.
39. King and Christou 2011, 454.
40. Ueda 2009; A. Louie 2004; Kibria 2002b.
41. A. Louie 2002, 313.
42. Kibria 2002b.
43. Tan 2014.
44. It should be noted that the PRC did offer dual citizenship up until 1955, when it was abolished in response to issues with overseas Chinese residents of Southeast Asia. See Thunø 2007.

45. Skrentny et al. 2007, 803.
46. Skrentny et al. 2007, 802–803.
47. Tu 1991, 22.
48. Wang, Tang, and Li 2015.
49. Ren and Liu 2018, 3.
50. See Hao and Welch 2012; Liu 2012; Kuah-Pearce, Eng, and Huang 2012.
51. Ministry of Education of the People's Republic of China 2018.
52. Chen 2017.
53. Chan and Tran 2011.
54. Jain 2013.
55. Yamashiro 2017.
56. Park and Chang 2005.
57. See appendix A for more detailed information about the research methods used for this study.
58. One of my participants resided in Xi'an, which is considered a second-tier Chinese city. This individual reached out to me directly to be interviewed upon learning of my research.
59. Santos and Harrell 2017.
60. Chang 2015.
61. BBC News 2019.
62. Ng 1998.
63. McCabe 2012.
64. L. K. Wang 2016.
65. Yamashiro 2017; Lee 2018.
66. Yamashiro 2017, 149.
67. Yamashiro 2017, 15.
68. Fechter 2016, 6.
69. Waters 1990.

Chapter 2   Growing Up In-Between

1. Fearnow 2018.
2. Song 2003, 36.
3. R. C. Smith 2002.
4. Levitt 2009, 1231.

5. V. Louie 2006.
6. Chao 1997.
7. M. Zhou 2009, 161.
8. M. Zhou 2009, 161.
9. V. Louie 2006, 363.
10. Pyke 2010.
11. Chou and Feagin 2015, 3–4.
12. Chou and Feagin 2015, 4.
13. This speaks to gendered stereotypes about Asian Americans that are fully explored in chapter 5.
14. U.S. Census Bureau 2019.
15. City of Cerritos 2017.
16. Trieu and Lee 2018, 68.
17. Kibria 2002a, 102.
18. Kiang, Witkow, and Thompson 2016, 1376.
19. Glick Schiller and Fouron 2002.
20. A. Louie 2002, 313.
21. Levitt 2009, 1226.
22. Kibria 2002a, 102.

Chapter 3   Creating the "Non-American American Dream" Overseas

1. Friedman 2011.
2. Greenhalgh and Winckler 2005.
3. Jain 2013, 896.
4. Levitt 2009, 1237.
5. Suh 2017, 317.
6. Ueda 2009, 84.
7. Hyun 2005.
8. Ascend 2017.
9. Ascend 2017.
10. Johnson and Sy 2016.
11. Chin 2016, 71.
12. Zippel 2017, 53.
13. Nagel 1994; Okamura 1981; Song 2003, 21.

14. Waters 1990; Alba 1990.
15. Kibria 2000, 80.
16. Gans 1979.
17. Tuan 1998.
18. Vasquez 2010, 46.
19. Jain 2011, 1320.
20. Jain 2011, 1320.
21. Jain 2011, 1321.
22. Wilson 2017.
23. Tsuda 2009, 24.

Chapter 4   Perpetually Chinese but Not Chinese Enough for China

1. V. Zheng 2017.
2. V. Zheng 2018.
3. V. Zheng 2018.
4. Yeoh and Willis 2005, 278.
5. Gold, Guthrie, and Wank 2002, 3.
6. Gold, Guthrie, and Wank 2002, 7.
7. Gold, Guthrie, and Wank 2002, 3.
8. Tu 1991.
9. Y. Zhou 2018b.
10. Y. Zhou 2018a.
11. M. Zuo 2018.
12. Fifield 2019.
13. Ip 2006, 61.
14. Zeithammer and Kellogg 2013.
15. M. Zuo 2018.
16. Yang 2015, 133.

Chapter 5   "Leftover Women" and "Kings of the Candy Shop"

1. Quora.com, n.d.
2. Crenshaw 1991.

3. Although I interviewed two female and one male LGBT+ individuals, their experiences differed greatly from those of my heterosexual participants. Thus, they are not incorporated into this particular analysis. However, it should be noted that none felt comfortable being open with their sexuality in China, reflecting the explicitly heteronormative atmosphere of the surrounding environment.

4. Chow, Segal, and Lin 2011, 3.

5. See Espiritu 2008; Eng 2001; Shek 2007.

6. Mahler and Pessar 2001.

7. For examples of articles on this topic, see Arieli 2007; L. K. Wang 2013.

8. See Fincher 2014; To 2015; To 2013.

9. Davis and Harrell 1993, 9.

10. Diamant 2000, 177.

11. Hershatter 2007, 61.

12. Hanser 2005, 581.

13. World Bank, n.d.

14. Tao 2017.

15. BBC News 2018.

16. Hochschild and Machung 2012.

17. J. Zuo 2013, 99.

18. Dasgupta, Matsumoto, and Xia 2015.

19. Cook and Dong 2011, 949.

20. Fincher 2013.

21. To 2015, 1.

22. Fincher 2014, 6.

23. SK-II Cosmetics 2016.

24. Ng and Nilsson 2014.

25. Greenhalgh 2008.

26. To, 2013, 2.

27. Sun 2017.

28. Zippel 2017.

29. H. K. Lee 2013, 37.

30. Eng 2001.

31. Suh 2016, 5–6.

32. Tajima 1989, 309.

33. Kim and Chung 2005, 76.

34. Espiritu 2008, 99.

35. See Qian and Lichter 2007; Qian and Lichter 2011.

36. W. Wang 2015.

37. Rudder 2014.

38. Robnett and Feliciano 2011.

39. Robnett and Feliciano 2011, 816.

40. Balistreri, Joyner, and Kao 2015.

41. Balistreri, Joyner, and Kao 2015, 729.

42. Fisman et al. 2008.

43. To understand this issue in Japan, see Kelsky 2001; for Taiwan, see Lan 2011; and for China, see Farrer 2010.

44. Lan 2011, 1672.

45. Farrer 2010, 91.

46. Cho 2012, 220.

47. Suh 2017.

48. Farrer, 2010.

49. T. Zheng 2006, 163.

50. Taylor and Napier 1996; Lan 2011; Farrer and Dale 2013; Napier and Taylor 2002.

51. Farrer and Dale 2013, 144.

52. Farrer and Dale 2013, 151.

53. To 2013.

54. Lee 2013.

55. Farrer and Dale 2013.

56. Taylor and Napier 1996, 79.

57. Sklair 2001.

58. M. Smith 2005, 236.

Chapter 6   Conclusion

1. Tu 1991, 4.

2. Viala-Gaudefroy and Lindaman 2020.

3. Redden 2020.

4. CBS7 2020.

5. Hong 2020.

6. Lowen Liu 2016.
7. Liu and Hahn 2020.
8. Y. N. Lee 2019.
9. Devlin, Silver, and Huang 2020.
10. Panda 2020.
11. Qin 2019.
12. Kuhn 2013.
13. Nordine 2018.
14. Raleigh 2019.

Appendix

1. Strauss and Corbin 1998.
2. Charmaz 2006.

References

Alba, Richard. 1990. *Ethnic Identity: The Transformation of White America.* New Haven, CT: Yale University Press.

Ambler, Pamela. 2017. "Asia Is Now Home to the Most Billionaires, with China Leading the Pack, Report Says." *Forbes,* October 30, 2017. www .forbes.com/sites/pamelaambler/2017/10/30/where-young-chinese -billionaires-are-making-their-wealth-and-spending-it/#3ab5543a7fb6.

Arieli, Daniella. 2007. "The Task of Being Content: Expatriate Wives in Beijing, Emotional Work and Patriarchal Bargain." *Journal of International Women's Studies* 8:18–31.

Ascend. 2017. "Race Trumps Gender in Silicon Valley's Double-Paned Glass Ceiling." News release, October 3, 2017. www.ascendleadership .org/news/369626/New-research-report-from-Ascend-Foundation-on -Silicon-Valley-leadership-diversity.htm.

Balistreri, Kelly Stamper, Kara Joyner, and Grace Kao. 2015. "Relationship Involvement among Young Adults: Are Asian American Men an Exceptional Case?" *Population Research and Policy Review* 34 (5): 709–732.

Basch, Linda, Nina Glick Schiller, and Christina Szanton Blanc, eds. 1994. *Nations Unbound: Transnational Projects, Postcolonial Predicaments, and Deterritorialized Nation States.* Langhorne, PA: Gordon and Breach.

BBC News. 2018. "China Dominates Self-Made Woman Rich List." March 8, 2018. www.bbc.com/news/business-43326764.

———. 2019. "What's behind the China-Taiwan Divide?" January 2, 2019. www.bbc.com/news/world-asia-34729538.

CBS7. 2020. "FBI Calling Stabbing at Midland Sam's a Hate Crime." March 30, 2020. www.cbs7.com/content/news/FBI-calling-stabbing-at -Midland-Sams-a-hate-crime-569233691.html.

Chan, Kwok Bun. 2005. *Chinese Identities, Ethnicity and Cosmopolitanism.* Hoboken, NJ: Routledge.

Chan, Yuk Wah, and Thi Le Thu Tran. 2011. "Recycling Migration and Changing Nationalisms: The Vietnamese Return Diaspora and Reconstruction of Vietnamese Nationhood." *Journal of Ethnic and Migration Studies* 37 (7): 1101–1117.

Chang, Bi-yu. 2015. *Place, Identity, and National Imagination in Postwar Taiwan.* Routledge Research on Taiwan 15. Hoboken, NJ: Routledge.

Chao, Theresa Hsu. 1997. "Chinese Heritage Community Language Schools in the United States." ERIC Digest, June 1997. https://eric.ed.gov/?id =ED409744.

Charmaz, Kathy C. 2006. *Constructing Grounded Theory: A Practical Guide through Qualitative Analysis.* Thousand Oaks, CA: Sage.

Chen, Te-Ping. 2017. "China Economy Draws More Students Back from Abroad." *Wall Street Journal,* March 1, 2017. www.wsj.com/articles /china-economy-draws-more-students-back-from-abroad-14883 64203.

Chin, Margaret M. 2016. "Asian Americans, Bamboo Ceilings, and Affirmative Action." *Contexts* 15 (1): 70–73.

Cho, John Song Pae. 2012. "Global Fatigue: Transnational Markets, Linguistic Capital, and Korean-American Male English Teachers in South Korea." *Journal of Sociolinguistics* 16 (2): 218–237.

Chou, Rosalind, and Joe Feagin. 2015. *Myth of the Model Minority: Asian Americans Facing Racism.* New York: Routledge.

Chow, Esther Ngan-ling, Marcia Texler Segal, and Tan Lin, eds. 2011. *Analyzing Gender, Intersectionality, and Multiple Inequalities: Global, Transnational and Local Contexts.* Bingley, UK: Emerald.

City of Cerritos. 2017. "Demographics." Race. Updated December 13, 2017. www.cerritos.us/NEWS_INFO/demographics.php#anchor3.

Cook, Sarah, and Xiao Yuan Dong. 2011. "Harsh Choices: Chinese Women's Paid Work and Unpaid Care Responsibilities under Economic Reform." *Development and Change* 42 (4): 947–965.

Crenshaw, Kimberle. 1991. "Mapping the Margins: Intersectionality, Identity Politics, and Violence against Women of Color." *Stanford Law Review* 43 (6): 1241–1299.

Dasgupta, Sukti, Makiko Matsumoto, and Cuntao Xia. 2015. "Women in the Labour Market in China." International Labour Office Asia-Pacific Working Paper Series.

Davis, Deborah, and Stevan Harrell. 1993. *Chinese Families in the Post-Mao Era*. Berkeley: University of California Press.

Devlin, Kat, Laura Silver, and Christine Huang. 2020. "U.S. Views of China Increasingly Negative amid Coronavirus Outbreak." Pew Research Center, April 21, 2020. www.pewresearch.org/global/2020/04 /21/u-s-views-of-china-increasingly-negative-amid-coronavirus -outbreak.

Diamant, Neil. 2000. "Re-examining the Impact of the 1950 Marriage Law: State Improvisation, Local Initiative and Rural Family Change." *China Quarterly* 161:171–198.

Dikötter, Frank. 2015. *The Discourse of Race in Modern China*. Oxford: Oxford University Press.

Echeverria-Estrada, Carlos, and Jeanne Batalova. 2020. "Chinese Immigrants in the United States." Migration Policy Institute, January 15, 2020. www.migrationinformation.org/feature/display.cfm?ID=876#1.

Eng, David L. 2001. *Racial Castration: Managing Masculinity in Asian America*. Durham, NC: Duke University Press.

Espiritu, Yen Le. 2008. *Asian American Women and Men: Labor, Laws, and Love*. Lanham, MD: Rowman & Littlefield.

Farrer, James. 2010. "A Foreign Adventurer's Paradise? Interracial Sexuality and Alien Sexual Capital in Reform Era Shanghai." *Sexualities* 13 (1): 69–95.

Farrer, James, and Sonja Dale. 2013. "Sexless in Shanghai: Gendered Mobility Strategies in a Transnational Sexual Field." In *Sexual Fields: Toward a Sociology of Collective Sexual Life*, edited by Adam Isaiah Green, 143–169. Chicago: University of Chicago Press.

Fearnow, Benjamin. 2018. "California College Counselor Blames 'Displacement of European-Americans' for Racist Video Rant." *Newsweek*, March 5, 2018. www.newsweek.com/golden-west-college-racist-video -rant-tony-kao-tarin-olson-counselor-european-830850.

Fechter, Anne-Meike. 2016. *Transnational Lives: Expatriates in Indonesia*. London: Routledge.

Fifield, Anna. 2019. "China Warns Students about 'Risks' of Going to the U.S. in the Latest Twist to the Trade War." *Washington Post*, June 3, 2019. www.washingtonpost.com/world/asia_pacific/china-warns-students -aboutrisks-of-going-to-the-us-in-the-latest-twist-to-the-trade-war/2019 /06/03/fbf8cc26-85f2-11e9-b1a8-716c9f3332ce_story.html.

Fincher, Leta Hong. 2013. "China's Entrenched Gender Gap." *New York Times*, May 20, 2013. www.nytimes.com/2013/05/21/opinion/global/chinas -entrenched-gender-gap.html.

———. 2014. *Leftover Women: The Resurgence of Gender Inequality in China*. London: Zed Books.

Fisman, Raymond, Sheena S. Iyengar, Emir Kamenica, and Itamar Simonson. 2008. "Racial Preferences in Dating." *Review of Economic Studies* 75 (1): 117–32.

Foner, Nancy. 2005. *In a New Land: A Comparative View of Immigration*. New York: New York University Press.

Friedman, Sophie. 2011. "U.S.-Born Chinese, Back in China to Set Up Shop." *Wall Street Journal*, November 10, 2011. www.wsj.com/articles/BL-SJB -8160.

Gans, Herbert J. 1979. "Symbolic Ethnicity: The Future of Ethnic Groups and Cultures in America." *Ethnic and Racial Studies* 2 (1): 1–20.

Gee, Buck, and Denise Peck. 2017. *The Illusion of Asian Success: Scant Progress for Minorities in Cracking the Glass Ceiling from 2007–2015*. Ascend Foundation, 2017. https://cdn.ymaws.com/www.ascendleadership .org/resource/resmgr/research/theillusionofasiansuccess.pdf.

Glick Schiller, Nina, and George Fouron. 2002. "Long-Distance National-ism Defined." In *The Anthropology of Politics: A Reader in Ethnography, Theory, and Critique*, edited by Joan Vincent, 356–365. Oxford: Blackwell.

Gold, Thomas, Doug Guthrie, and David Wank, eds. 2002. *Social Connections in China: Institutions, Culture, and the Changing Nature of Guanxi*. Structural Analysis in the Social Sciences 21. Cambridge: Cambridge University Press.

Greenhalgh, Susan. 2008. *Just One Child: Science and Policy in Deng's China*. Berkeley: University of California Press.

Greenhalgh, Susan, and Edwin A. Winckler. 2005. *Governing China's Population: From Leninist to Neoliberal Biopolitics*. Palo Alto, CA: Stanford University Press.

Hanser, Amy. 2005. "The Gendered Rice Bowl: The Sexual Politics of Service Work in Urban China." *Gender and Society* 19 (5): 581–600.

Hao, Jie, and Anthony Welch. 2012. "A Tale of Sea Turtles: Job-Seeking Experiences of Hai Gui (High-Skilled Returnees) in China." *High Education Policy* 25 (2): 243–260.

Hernandez, Javier, and Quoctrung Bui. 2018. "The American Dream Is Alive. In China." *New York Times*, November 18, 2018. www.nytimes .com/interactive/2018/11/18/world/asia/china-social-mobility.html.

Hershatter, Gail. 2007. *Women in China's Long Twentieth Century*. Berkeley: University of California Press.

Hochschild, Arlie, and Anne Machung. 2012. *The Second Shift: Working Families and the Revolution at Home*. New York: Penguin.

Hong, Cathy Park. 2020. "The Slur I Never Expected to Hear in 2020." *New York Times Magazine*, April 12, 2020. www.nytimes.com/2020/04 /12/magazine/asian-american-discrimination-coronavirus.html.

Hyun, Jane. 2005. *Breaking the Bamboo Ceiling: Career Strategies for Asians*. New York: HarperBusiness.

Ip, Manying. 2006. "Returnees and Transnationals: Evolving Identities of Chinese (PRC) Immigrants in New Zealand." *Journal of Population Studies* 33:61–102.

Jain, Sonali. 2011. "The Rights of 'Return': Ethnic Identities in the Workplace among Second-Generation Indian-American Professionals in the Parental Homeland." *Journal of Ethnic and Migration Studies* 37 (9): 1313–1330.

———. 2013. "For Love and Money: Second-Generation Indian-Americans 'Return' to India." *Ethnic and Racial Studies* 36 (5): 896–914.

Johnson, Stefanie K., and Thomas Sy. 2016. "Why Aren't There More Asian Americans in Leadership Positions?" *Harvard Business Review*, December 19, 2016. https://hbr.org/2016/12/why-arent-there-more-asian -americans-in-leadership-positions.

Kawai, Yuko. 2005. "Stereotyping Asian Americans: The Dialectic of the Model Minority and the Yellow Peril." *Howard Journal of Communications* 16 (2): 109–130.

Kelsky, Karen. 2001. *Women on the Verge: Japanese Women, Western Dreams*. Durham, NC: Duke University Press.

Kiang, Lisa, Melissa R. Witkow, and Taylor L. Thompson. 2016. "Model Minority Stereotyping, Perceived Discrimination, and Adjustment among Adolescents from Asian American Backgrounds." *Journal of Youth and Adolescence* 45 (7): 1366–1379.

Kibria, Nazli. 2000. "Race, Ethnic Options, and Ethnic Binds: Identity Negotiations of Second-Generation Chinese and Korean Americans." *Sociological Perspectives* 43 (1): 77–95.

———. 2002a. *Becoming Asian American*. Baltimore, MD: Johns Hopkins University Press.

———. 2002b. "Of Blood, Belonging, and Homeland Trips: Transnationalism and Identity among Second-Generation Chinese and Korean Americans." In *The Changing Face of Home: The Transnational Lives of the Second Generation*, edited by Peggy Levitt and Mary C. Waters, 295–311. New York: Russell Sage Foundation.

Kim, Minjeong, and Angie Y. Chung. 2005. "Consuming Orientalism: Images of Asian/American Women in Multicultural Advertising." *Qualitative Sociology* 28 (1): 67–91.

King, Russell, and Anastasia Christou. 2011. "Of Counter-Diaspora and Reverse Transnationalism: Return Mobilities to and from the Ancestral Homeland." *Mobilities* 6 (4): 451–466.

Kochhar, Rakesh, and Anthony Cilluffo. 2018. "Income Inequality in the U.S. Is Rising Most Rapidly among Asians." Pew Research Center, July 12, 2018. www.pewsocialtrends.org/2018/07/12/income-inequality-in -the-u-s-is-rising-most-rapidly-among-asians.

Kuah-Pearce, Khun Eng, and Yedan Huang. 2012. "'Talent Circulators' in Shanghai: Return Migrants and their Strategies for Success." *Globalization, Societies and Education* 13 (2): 276–294.

Kuhn, Robert Lawrence. 2013. "Understanding the Chinese Dream." *China Daily*, July 19, 2013. http://usa.chinadaily.com.cn/opinion/2013 -07/19/content_16814756.htm.

Lan, Pei-Chia. 2011. "White Privilege, Language Capital and Cultural Ghettoisation: Western High-Skilled Migrants in Taiwan." *Journal of Ethnic and Migration Studies* 37 (10): 1669–1693.

Lee, Helene K. 2013. "'I'm My Mother's Daughter, I'm My Husband's Wife, I'm My Child's Mother, I'm Nothing Else': Resisting Traditional Korean Roles as Korean American Working Women in Seoul, South Korea." *Women's Studies International Forum* 36:37–43.

————. 2018. *Between Foreign and Family: Return Migration and Identity Construction among Korean Americans and Korean Chinese.* New Brunswick: Rutgers University Press.

Lee, Yen Nee. 2019. "These 4 Charts Show How US-China Trade Has Changed during the Tariff Dispute." CNBC, September 16, 2019. www.cnbc.com/2019/09/18/what-us-china-trade-war-means-for-imports-exports-and-soybeans.html.

Levitt, Peggy. 2009. "Roots and Routes: Understanding the Lives of the Second Generation Transnationally." *Journal of Ethnic and Migration Studies* 35 (7): 1225–1242.

Ley, David, and Audrey Kobayashi. 2005. "Back to Hong Kong: Return Migration or Transnational Sojourn?" *Global Networks* 5 (2): 111–127.

Lin, Monica H., Virginia S. Y. Kwan, Anna Cheung, and Susan T. Fiske. 2005. "Stereotype Content Model Explains Prejudice for an Envied Outgroup: Scale of Anti-Asian American Stereotypes." *Personality and Social Psychology Bulletin* 31 (1): 34–47.

Liu, Kelsey, and Monica Hahn. 2020. "The Asian American Reply to Pandemic-Era Racism Must Be Cross-Racial Solidarity." Truthout, May 31, 2020. https://truthout.org/articles/the-asian-american-reply-to-pandemic-era-racism-must-be-cross-racial-solidarity.

Liu, Lisong. 2012. "Return Migration and Selective Citizenship: A Study of Returning Chinese Professional Migrants from the United States." *Journal of Asian American Studies* 15 (1): 35–68.

Liu, Lowen. 2016. "Just the Wrong Amount of American: Wen Ho Lee's 1999 Arrest Taught Chinese Americans That Their Country May Never Trust Them." *Slate*, September 11, 2016. www.slate.com/articles/news_and_politics/the_next_20/2016/09/the_case_of_scientist_wen_ho_lee_and_chinese_americans_under_suspicion_for.html.

Louie, Andrea. 2002. "Creating Histories for the Present: Second-Generation (Re)definitions of Chinese American Culture." In *The Changing Face of Home: The Transnational Lives of the Second Generation*, edited by Peggy Levitt and Mary C. Waters, 312–340. New York: Russell Sage Foundation.

————. 2004. *Chineseness across Borders: Renegotiating Chinese Identities in China and the United States.* Durham, NC: Duke University Press.

Louie, Vivian. 2006. "Growing Up Ethnic in Transnational Worlds: Identities among Second-Generation Chinese and Dominicans." *Identities: Global Studies in Culture and Power* 13 (3): 363–394.

Mahler, Sarah, and Patricia Pessar. 2001. "Gendered Geographies of Power: Analyzing Gender across Transnational Spaces." *Identities* 7:441–459.

Marsh, Natalie. 2017. "China Sees 11% Growth of International Student Enrolments." Pie News, March 28, 2017. https://thepienews.com/news /china-11-percent-growth-international-student.

McCabe, Kristen. 2012. "Taiwanese Immigrants in the United States in 2010." Migration Policy Institute, January 31, 2012. www.migration policy.org/article/taiwanese-immigrants-united-states.

Ministry of Education of the People's Republic of China. 2018. "2017 Sees Increase in Number of Chinese Students Studying Abroad and Returning after Studies." April 3, 2018. http://en.moe.gov.cn/News /Top_News/201804/t20180404_332354.html.

Nagel, Joane. 1994. "Constructing Ethnicity: Creating and Recreating Ethnic Identity and Culture." *Social Problems* 41 (1): 152–176.

Napier, Nancy, and Sully Taylor. 2002. "Experiences of Women Professionals Abroad: Comparisons Across Japan, China and Turkey." *International Journal of Human Resource Management* 13 (5): 837–851.

National Bureau of Statistics of China. 2011. "Major Figures on Residents from Hong Kong, Macao and Taiwan and Foreigners Covered by 2010 Population Census." April 29, 2011. www.stats.gov.cn/english/NewsEvents /201104/t20110429_26451.html.

Ng, Franklin. 1998. *The Taiwanese Americans*. Westport, CT: Greenwood Press.

Ng, Valerie, and Erik Nilsson. 2014. "Much Ado about *Shengnu*," *China Daily*, February 12, 2014. http://usa.chinadaily.com.cn/epaper/2014-02 /12/content_17279212.htm.

Nordine, Michael. 2018. "As China Dominates the Global Box Office, a Look at the Movies Giving Hollywood a Run for Its Money." IndieWire, April 30, 2018. www.indiewire.com/2018/04/chinese-box -office-wolf-warrior-2-1201956049.

Okamura, Jonathan Y. 1981. "Situational Ethnicity." *Ethnic and Racial Studies* 4 (4): 452–465.

Ong, Aihwa. 1999. *Flexible Citizenship: The Cultural Logics of Transnationality.* Durham, NC: Duke University Press.

Panda, Ankit. 2020. "Survey: Chinese Report Less Favorable Views of US Democracy." *Diplomat,* April 9, 2020. https://thediplomat.com/2020/04/survey-chinese-report-less-favorable-views-of-us-democracy.

Park, Jung-Sun, and Paul Y. Chang. 2005. "Contention in the Construction of a Global Korean Community: The Case of the Overseas Korean Act." *Journal of Korean Studies* 10 (1): 1–27.

Pew Research Center Social and Demographic Trends. 2017. "Chinese in the U.S. Fact Sheet." Pew Research Center, September 8, 2017. www.pewsocialtrends.org/fact-sheet/asian-americans-chinese-in-the-u-s.

Portes, Alejandro, and Min Zhou. 2012. "The New Second Generation: Segmented Assimilation and Its Variants." In *The New Immigration: An Interdisciplinary Reader,* edited by Marcelo Suárez-Orozco, Carola Suárez-Orozco, and Desirée Baolian Qin, 99–116. New York: Routledge.

Purkayastha, Bandana. 2005. *Negotiating Ethnicity: Second-Generation South Asians Traverse a Transnational World.* New Brunswick, NJ: Rutgers University Press.

Pyke, Karen D. 2010. "What Is Internalized Racial Oppression and Why Don't We Study It? Acknowledging Racism's Hidden Injuries." *Sociological Perspectives* 53 (4): 551–572.

Qian, Zhenchao, and Daniel T. Lichter. 2007. "Social Boundaries and Marital Assimilation: Interpreting Trends in Racial and Ethnic Intermarriage." *American Sociological Review* 72 (1): 68–94.

———. 2011. "Changing Patterns of Interracial Marriage in a Multiracial Society." *Journal of Marriage and Family* 73 (5): 1065–1084.

Qin, Amy. 2019. "To Many Chinese, America Was Like 'Heaven.' Now They're Not So Sure." *New York Times,* May 18, 2019. www.nytimes.com/2019/05/18/world/asia/china-america-trade.html.

Quora.com. n.d. "What Is It Like to Be an ABC (aka an American Born Chinese) Living in China?" Accessed June 5, 2018. www.quora.com/What-is-it-like-to-be-an-ABC-aka-an-American-Born-Chinese-living-in-China.

Raleigh, Helen. 2019. "*Wolf Warrior II* Tells Us a Lot about China." *National Review,* July 20, 2019. www.nationalreview.com/2019/07/wolf-warrior-ii-tells-us-a-lot-about-china.

Redden, Elizabeth. 2020. "Scholars v. COVID-19 Racism." Inside Higher
Ed, April 2, 2020. www.insidehighered.com/news/2020/04/02/scholars
-confront-coronavirus-related-racism-classroom-research-and
-community.

Ren, Na, and Hong Liu. 2018. "Domesticating 'Transnational Cultural
Capital': The Chinese State and Diasporic Technopreneur Returnees."
Journal of Ethnic and Migration Studies 45 (13): 1–20.

Robnett, Belinda, and Cynthia Feliciano. 2011. "Patterns of Racial-Ethnic
Exclusion by Internet Daters." *Social Forces* 89 (3): 807–828.

Rudder, Christian. 2014. "Race and Attraction, 2009–2014." OkCupid
.com, September 10, 2014. www.gwern.net/docs/psychology/okcupid
/raceandattraction20092014.html.

Santos, Gonçalo, and Stevan Harrell. 2017. *Transforming Patriarchy:
Chinese Families in the Twenty-First Century.* Seattle: University of
Washington Press.

Schiller, Nina Glick, Linda Basch, and Cristina Blanc-Szanton. 1992.
"Transnationalism: A New Analytic Framework for Understanding
Migration." *Annals of the New York Academy of Sciences* 645 (1): 1–24.

Schmitz, Rob. 2017. "Who's Lifting Chinese People Out of Poverty?"
National Public Radio, January 17, 2017. www.npr.org/sections
/goatsandsoda/2017/01/17/509521619/whos-lifting-chinese-people-out-of
-poverty.

Shek, Yen Ling. 2007. "Asian American Masculinity: A Review of the
Literature." *Journal of Men's Studies* 14 (3): 379–391.

Sklair, Leslie. 2001. *The Transnational Capitalist Class.* Oxford: Blackwell.

Skrentny, John D., Stephanie Chan, Jon Fox, and Denis Kim. 2007.
"Defining Nations in Asia and Europe: A Comparative Analysis of
Ethnic Return Migration Policy." *International Migration Review* 41
(4): 793–825.

SK-II Cosmetics. 2016. "SK-II: Marriage Market Takeover." Posted
April 6, 2016. YouTube video, 4:16. www.youtube.com/watch?v
=irfd74z52Cw.

Smith, Michael. 2005. "Transnational Urbanism Revisited." *Journal of
Ethnic and Migration Studies* 31 (2): 235–244.

Smith, Robert C. 2002. "Life Course, Generation, and Social Location as
Factors Shaping Second-Generation Transnational Life." In *The*

Changing Face of Home: The Transnational Lives of the Second Generation, edited by Peggy Levitt and Mary C. Waters, 145–167. New York: Russell Sage Foundation.

Song, Miri. 2003. *Choosing Ethnic Identity*. Cambridge: Polity Press.

Strauss, Anselm, and Juliet Corbin. 1998. *Basics of Qualitative Research: Techniques and Procedures for Developing Grounded Theory*. Thousand Oaks, CA: Sage.

Suh, Stephen Cho. 2017. "Negotiating Masculinity across Borders: A Transnational Examination of Korean American Masculinities." *Men and Masculinities* 20 (3): 317–344.

Sun, Wanning. 2017. "'My Parents Say Hurry Up and Find a Girl': China's Millions of Lonely 'Leftover Men.'" *The Guardian*, September 28, 2017. www.theguardian.com/inequality/2017/sep/28/my-parents-say-hurry-up-and-find-a-girl-chinas-millions-of-lonely-leftover-men.

Tajima, Renee E. 1989. "Lotus Blossoms Don't Bleed: Images of Asian Women." *Making Waves: An Anthology of Writings by and about Asian American Women*, edited by Asian Women United of California, 308–317. Boston: Beacon Press.

Tan, Weiyun. 2014. "More Foreigners Coming to Live in China." *Shanghai Daily*, June 2, 2014. http://en.people.cn/n/2014/0602/c90882-8735618.html.

Tao, Li. 2017. "They Hold Up Half the Sky: Six of Every 10 of the World's Self-Made, Women Billionaires Are in China." *South China Morning Post*, October 26, 2017. www.scmp.com/business/china-business/article/2117158/china-has-most-self-made-women-billionaires-globally.

Taylor, Sully, and Nancy Napier. 1996. "Working in Japan: Lessons from Women Expatriates." *MIT Sloan Management Review* 37 (3): 76–84.

Thunø, Mette, ed. 2007. *Beyond Chinatown: New Chinese Migration and the Global Expansion of China*. NIAS Studies in Asian Topics 41. Copenhagen: NIAS Press.

To, Sandy. 2013. "Understanding *Sheng Nu* ('Leftover Women'): The Phenomenon of Late Marriage among Chinese Professional Women." *Symbolic Interaction* 36 (1): 1–20.

———. 2015. *China's Leftover Women: Late Marriage among Professional Women and Its Consequences*. Abingdon, UK: Routledge.

Trading Economics. n.d. "China GDP Annual Growth Rate." Accessed July 1, 2018. https://tradingeconomics.com/china/gdp-growth-annual.

Trieu, Monica M., and Hana C. Lee. 2018. "Asian Americans and Internalized Racial Oppression: Identified, Reproduced, and Dismantled." *Sociology of Race and Ethnicity* 4 (1): 67–82.

Tsuda, Takeyuki. 2009. *Diasporic Homecomings: Ethnic Return Migration in Comparative Perspective.* Stanford, CA: Stanford University Press.

Tu, Weiming. 1991. "Cultural China: The Periphery as the Center." *Daedalus* 120 (2): 1–32.

Tuan, Mia. 1998. *Forever Foreigners or Honorary Whites? The Asian Ethnic Experience Today.* New Brunswick, NJ: Rutgers University Press.

Ueda, Naho. 2009. "Chinese Americans in China: Ethnicity, Transnationalism, and Roots Tourism." PhD diss., Texas A&M University. ProQuest (UMI Dissertations Publishing).

U.S. Census Bureau. 2019. "Quick Facts: Queens County (Queens Borough), New York." Accessed November 12, 2019. www.census.gov /quickfacts/fact/table/queenscountyqueensboroughnewyork/PST 040218#PST040218.

Vasquez, Jessica. 2010. "Blurred Borders for Some but Not 'Others': Racialization, 'Flexible Ethnicity,' Gender, and Third-Generation Mexican American Identity." *Sociological Perspectives* 53 (1): 45–71.

Viala-Gaudefroy, Jérôme, and Dana Lindaman. 2020. "Donald Trump's 'Chinese Virus': The Politics of Naming." *The Conversation,* April 21, 2020. https://theconversation.com/donald-trumps-chinese -virus-the-politics-of-naming-136796.

Waldinger, Roger. 2015. *The Cross-Border Connection: Immigrants, Emigrants, and Their Homelands.* Cambridge, MA: Harvard University Press.

Wang, Leslie K. 2013. "Unequal Logics of Care: Gender, Globalization, and Volunteer Work of Expatriate Wives in China." *Gender and Society* 27 (4): 538–560.

———. 2016. "The Benefits of In-Betweenness: Return Migration of Second-Generation Chinese American Professionals to China." *Journal of Ethnic and Migration Studies* 42 (12): 1941–1958.

Wang, L. Ling-chi. 1991. "Roots and Changing Identity of the Chinese in the United States." *Daedalus* 120 (2): 181–206.

Wang, Qingfang, Li Tang, and Huiping Li. 2015. "Return Migration of the Highly Skilled in Higher Education Institutions: A Chinese University Case." *Population, Space and Place* 21 (8): 771–787.

Wang, Wendy. 2015. "Interracial Marriage: Who Is Marrying Out?" Pew Research Center, June 12, 2015. www.pewresearch.org/fact-tank/2015 /06/12/interracial-marriage-who-is-marrying-out.

Waters, Mary C. 1990. *Ethnic Options: Choosing Identities in America.* Berkeley: University of California Press.

Wike, Richard, and Kat Devlin. 2018. "As Trade Tensions Rise, Fewer Americans See China Favorably." Pew Research Center, August 28, 2018. www.pewglobal.org/2018/08/28/as-trade-tensions-rise-fewer-americans -see-china-favorably.

Wilson, Reid. 2017. "More Americans Have College Degrees Than Ever Before." *The Hill*, April 3, 2017. http://thehill.com/homenews/state -watch/326995-census-more-americans-have-college-degrees-than-ever -before.

World Bank. n.d. "Labor Force Participation Rate, Female (% of Female Population Ages 15+) (Modeled ILO Estimate)." Accessed June 17, 2018. https://data.worldbank.org/indicator/SL.TLF.CACT.FE.ZS ?locations=CN.

Yam, Kimberly. 2017. "Asian-Americans Have Highest Poverty Rate in NYC, but Stereotypes Make the Issue Invisible." *Huffington Post*, May 8, 2017. www.huffingtonpost.com/entry/asian-american-poverty-nyc _us_58ff7f40e4b0c46f0782a5b6.

Yamashiro, Jane. 2017. *Redefining Japaneseness: Japanese Americans in the Ancestral Homeland.* New Brunswick, NJ: Rutgers University Press.

Yang, Dennis. 2015. *The Pursuit of the Chinese Dream in America: Chinese Undergraduate Students at American Universities.* Lanham, MD: Rowman & Littlefield.

Yeoh, Brenda S. A., and Katie Willis. 2005. "Singaporean and British Transmigrants in China and the Cultural Politics of 'Contact Zones.'" *Journal of Ethnic and Migration Studies: Ordinary and Middling Transnationalisms* 31 (2): 269–285.

Yoo, Hyung Chol, Kimberly S. Burrola, and Michael F. Steger. 2010. "A Preliminary Report on a New Measure: Internalization of the Model Minority Myth Measure (IM-4) and Its Psychological Correlates among Asian American College Students." *Journal of Counseling Psychology* 57 (1): 114–127.

Zeithammer, Robert, and Ryan P. Kellogg. 2013. "The Hesitant *Hai Gui*: Return-Migration Preferences of US-Educated Chinese Scientists and Engineers." *Journal of Marketing Research* 50 (5): 644–663.

Zheng, Tiantian. 2006. "Cool Masculinity: Male Clients' Sex Consumption and Business Alliance in Urban China's Sex Industry." *Journal of Contemporary China* 15 (46): 161–182.

Zheng, Victor. 2017. "Our Prejudice: A Documentary on Chinese and Their Overseas Counterparts." Posted June 11, 2017. YouTube video, 19:55. www.youtube.com/watch?v=c3InJ9w3Koo.

———. 2018. "Can a Chinese-American Be Chinese and American? (Part 2)." RADII, January 18, 2018. https://radiichina.com/can-a-chinese -american-be-chinese-and-american-part-2.

Zhou, Min. 2009. *Contemporary Chinese America: Immigration, Ethnicity, and Community Transformation*. Philadelphia: Temple University Press.

Zhou, Youyou. 2018a. "The Impact of Chinese Students in the US, Charted and Mapped." Quartz, October 2, 2018. https://qz.com /1410768/the-number-of-chinese-students-in-the-us-charted-and -mapped.

———. 2018b. "Top Countries of Citizenship for Foreign Students in the US." Quartz, July 2018. www.theatlas.com/charts/SJQL4Q-9Q.

Zippel, Kathrin. 2017. *Women in Global Science: Advancing Academic Careers through International Collaboration*. Palo Alto, CA: Stanford University Press.

Zuo, Jiping. 2013. "Women's Liberation and Gender Obligation Equality in Urban China: Work/Family Experiences of Married Individuals in the 1950s." *Science and Society* 77 (1): 98–125.

Zuo, Mandy. 2018. "Why China's Overseas Students Find Things Aren't Always Better Back Home." *South China Morning Post*, September 1, 2018. www.scmp.com/news/china/society/article/2162229/why-chinas -overseas-students-find-things-arent-always-better-back.

Index

Page numbers in *italic* indicate a table.

ABC men: emasculating racialized
stereotypes in United States, 107–108,
126; experiences of dating, 109–115;
increased status of, 99; LBH (losers
back home) concept, 113; Peter Pan
syndrome, 113; reversal of romantic
desirability in ethnic homeland,
107–109; romantic options in ancestral
homeland, 126. *See also* gendered
experiences in ancestral homeland
ABCs (American-born Chinese):
Chinese American identity of, 5–7, 13;
Chinese incentives to attract Western
talent, 17–19; defined, 2; denial of
recognition, 7; effects of immersion in
Chinese society, 123; forever foreign
in United States, 10–13; future
migrations of, 134; in-betweenness of
lived experiences, 7; later generations
of, 73; leveraging of social ambiguity,
124; as *meiji huaren*, 17; overview, 1–5,
22–23; performing flexible identities
in China, 13–15; perpetual Chinese in
PRC, 10–13; relocation reasons, 6;
returning to China, 8–9; second-
generation ancestral homeland
migration, 15–17; use of strategic
in-betweenness, 14. *See also* ABC
men; ABC women
ABC women: dating and marriage
practices of, 15; diminished options in

ancestral homeland, 126; downward
sexual mobility of, 115–120; gender
egalitarianism at work, 104–107;
hypersexual racialized stereotypes in
United States, 108; as leftover women
(*sheng nü*), 99, 102–104; managing
marginalization through migration,
120–121; on men's experience of
dating, 112–113; need to prioritize
career or personal life, 126; reversal of
romantic desirability in ethnic
homeland, 107–109; social distancing
from local women, 118. *See also*
gendered experiences in ancestral
homeland; marriage
Africa, China's international influence
in, 132, 133
African Americans, 11, 26, 37, 43, 63, 131
Alan (participant), 59–60, 93–94, 132–133
American (*meiguoren*) (term), Chinese
concept of, 3
American/Chinese dichotomy: author's
experiences with, 2; in China, 7, 95,
124; cultural knowledge and, 83;
gendered expectations and, 24;
language fluency and, 83, 89;
limitations of, 76; as social capital, 79.
See also model minority/perpetual
foreigner dichotomy
American citizenship: downplaying
privilege of, 106; leveraging, 4

163

image, 134; U.S. emigration from, 9; U.S. immigration quotas, 20; Xi Jinping, 9, 132 education: ABCs on U.S. education system, 72; Chinese Americans' privilege and, 6; Chinese education critiques, 70–71, 72; Chinese student returnees, 18, 90–95; educational migrants, 27–28; ethnic collectivity and, 40–44; overseas educated *haigui*, 125; study abroad in young adulthood, 44–47; U.S. college education statistics, 72

egalitarianism, 99, 104–107

elite migrants: ABCs as, 123; flexible ethnicity performance by, 124; strategic in-betweenness deployment by, 124

Ellen (participant), 31, 51, 67, 119

Elsa (participant), 45

emotional belonging: dislocation experience, 16; economic issues and, 50–57; lack of, 7; returning to ancestral homeland and, 7, 16, 32; seeking in China, 1, 6

equality, as American idea, 67–68

Eric (participant), 59; advantages in Chinese economy, 133

ethnic belonging: blood ties and, 7; depth of sense of, 5, 123. *See also* blood-based belonging; emotional belonging

ethnic collectivity, 40–44

ethnic enclaves, 10, 38–40

ethnic flexibility, 62–65

ethnic heritage: cultural pride, 40–44; downplaying of, 3, 32–35, 47; ethnic enclaves and, 10, 38–40; flexible ethnicity, 62–65, 66; relocation to ethnic homeland, 123; sense of belonging and identification with, 13; shifts between ethnic options, 124

ethnic identity: categories of belonging and, 15; effects on, 6; performative nature of, 13–14

ethnicity (term), 7, 13

ethnic majority, being part of, 123

exemplary minority status. *See* model minority/perpetual foreigner dichotomy

Farewell, The (2019 film) (Wang), 129

Farrer, James, 110, 113

Feagin, Joe, 33

Fincher, Leta Hong, 102

first-generation migrants: relocations of, 15; terminology, 22; transnational ties and, 27

flexible ethnicity, 14, 62–65, 124

foreigner/native dichotomy, 78, 95, 124; author's experiences of, 3; in China, 7, 8, 11–13, 17–19, 22, 49; in gendered experiences, 24; language fluency and, 89; limitations of, 76; as social capital, 79; strategic use of, 64–65; in United States, 10–11. *See also* American/Chinese dichotomy; gendered experiences in ancestral homeland; *haigui*

free trade, 9

Fujianese, 19

gendered experiences in ancestral homeland: ABC men's dating experiences in PRC, 109–115; ABC women's downward sexual mobility, 115–119; gender egalitarianism at work, 104–107; gender relations in PRC, 100–104; managing marginalization through migration, 120–121; overview, 6, 24, 97–100, 121–122; reversal of romantic desirability in ethnic homeland, 107–109. *See also* ABC men; ABC women; dating and marriage practices

gender issues: heteronormativity, 19; intersectionality and, 126; in PRC, 100–104; of privileged migration, 98–99; in South Korea, 106

George (participant), 32, 54, 85, 114–115, 118

glass ceiling effect, 126

global capitalism, 8, 9, 11, 23, 123, 134

Gold, Thomas, 87

guanxi (social connections), 87–88

Guthrie, Doug, 87

Hahn, Monica, 131
haigui (overseas returnees), 18, 95;
    competition from, 24, 77, 90–95;
    overseas educated, 125; political
    situation and, 91
Henry (participant), 30
heteronormativity, 19, 146n3
heterosexual men: dating and marriage
    practices of, 14–15; elevated global
    status of, 126
Hong, Cathy Park, 130
Hong Kong: Cantonese language in,
    29, 30; Chinese people in United
    States from, 9; culturally Chinese as
    being from, 31; early homeland trips
    with family to, 31; mainland Chinese
    rule in, 2; relocation between
    Vancouver and, 15; second-generation
    ABCs, 141n3; U.S. emigration
    from, 9
Howard (participant), 39, 55–57, 74
Hu, Austin, 49
huaqiao (PRC-born individuals), 17, 18
huaren (overseas descendants), 13
huayi/huaren (diasporic Chinese),
    13, 17, 76
hybrid nature of lived experiences, 7, 26,
    76, 81, 124
hypervisibility as Chinese American,
    129–131

identity: identity-based issues
    resolution, 7, 125; immersion in
    Chinese society and, 123; as ongoing
    construct, 124; in United States,
    25–48
Ilene (participant), 87–88
immigration: Asian Exclusion Act of
    1924, 107; Chinese Exclusion Act
    of 1882, 107; PRC quotas, 20; U.S.
    Immigration and Nationality Act of
    1965, 10
in-betweenness, 25–48; of ABCs' lived
    experiences, 7; connecting to roots,
    44–47; early experiences of race and

racism, 33–37; early homeland trips
    with family, 30–32; effect of China's
    global ascendance on strategic, 134;
    from ethnic ambivalence to pride in
    young adulthood, 40–44; ethnic and
    racial ambivalence in childhood and
    adolescence, 32–33; ethnic enclaves as
    centers of identity and belonging,
    38–40; independent travel in young
    adulthood, 44–47; leveraging of for
    career success, 128; limits of, 81–83;
    maintaining language, 28–30;
    overview, 23, 25–27, 47–48; parental
    lessons on cultural pride, 37–38;
    reconciling with China/Chinese
    culture, 129; strategic deployment of
    by elite migrants, 124; study abroad
    in young adulthood, 44–47;
    transnational childhoods, 27–28
income, Chinese American's privilege
    and, 6; income inequality, 10, 77
Indian Americans, 36, 51–52, 69
individualism, American, 67, 70
inequality of gender in PRC, 100–104
insider/outsider dichotomy, 7, 14, 63, 65,
    95, 104
intersectionality, 126
invisibility as Chinese American,
    129–131

Jain, Sonali, 52, 69
James (participant), 43–44
Japan: English teachers in, 21; foreign
    national visas in, 18–19; marital
    statistics for women in, 103; survey on
    women professionals, 120
Jason (participant), 70
Jeff (participant), 71
Jenny (participant), 42–43, 105, 127
jia laowai (fake foreigners), 89
Joanne (participant), 28–29, 37–38, 118
Jonathan (participant), 41–42, 46, 54–55,
    61, 83, 95, 104–105, 111–112, 128
Joy (participant), 38, 52, 82, 112, 116, 121
Julia (participant), 34–35

migration: circular migration patterns, 15; managing marginalization through, 120–121; strategic switching, 15
model minority myth, 10–11, 23, 32–33, 42–44, 129, 131
model minority/perpetual foreigner dichotomy, 10–13, 26, 32–33, 77, 123
Monica (participant), 78–79, 82

Nagel, Joanne, 13
Natalie (participant), 119
non-Westerner/Westener dichotomy, 124
North Korea, 9

One-Child Policy, 103–104
overcrowding, 6
overseas descendants (*huaren*), 13

Parasite (2020 film) (Bong), 129
parental homeland, navigation of norms of, 124
patriarchal norms, heterosexual men and, 126
patriotism, renewal of, 132
Paul (participant), 65–66, 80, 117
Peck, Denise, 57
people of color, 10, 26, 33, 35, 38, 131
perpetual Chinese in PRC, 24, 33, 123; dealing with questions of origin, 77–81; downsides of, 81–83; expectations of cultural knowledge, 85–90; expectations of cultural understanding, 83–85; expectations of language fluency, 83–85; heightened competition with *haigui* returnees, 90–95; overview, 11–13, 23, 75–77, 95–96
perpetual foreigner in United States, 123
Peter Pan syndrome, 113
Philip (participant), 62, 64–65
public opinion: negative views of China, 131–132; negative views of United States, 131–132

quality of life concerns, 6; environmental pollution, 127; limited educational options for children, 127
Quora.com survey on dating, 97–98

racial belonging: blood ties and, 7; depth of sense of, 5, 123; pro/cons of racial divisions, 83, 89, 95, 96; racial boundaries, 7
racial identity, effects on, 6; fluidity of, 124; identity-based issues resolution, 125–126; intersectionality and, 126
racial marginalization: downplaying of, 130; model minority label and, 10; shared experiences of, 42; solidarity and, 131
racist discourse, 129–130; Black-white relations, 11, 26, 37, 42–43; COVID-19 and, 129–130; on exemplary minority status, 10; negative stereotypes, 26–27, 57–58; race (term), defined, 7; racial and ethnic exclusion, 33–37; white privilege, 129; white supremacy, 129; xenophobia, 37, 78, 129; Yellow Peril representations, 8–9, 24, 129
Raleigh, Helen, 133
reciprocal obligations, 87–88
relocations, 126
remainees, factors pushing them out of country, 127
Ren, Na, 18
research methodology, 135–136; gender, 136, *136*; methods, 19–21; participant demographics, 72–73, *136*; participants, 5–6, 19–21, 146n3; relocations, 126; remainees, 127; respondents, 126–127; returnees to United States, 126; return migrants, 123; software and coding system, 137; terminology, 21–22. *See also specific participants*
return migrants: defined, 21–22; emotional belonging and, 7; reason for, 123; returnees to United States, 126
Richard (participant), 31, 36, 89, 109

Robert (participant), 28
Roger (participant), 94
roots tourism: ambivalence toward, 51,
54, 56, 73; cultural connections and,
125; early homeland trips with family,
31; homeland travel and, 16–17;
Mandarin (language) and, 125; study
abroad in young adulthood, 44–47, 73

Sarah (participant), 91
second-generation ABCs: ancestral
homeland migration of, 15–16;
defined, 141n3; early homeland trips
with family and, 32; effect of China's
global ascendance on, 134; identity-
based issues of, 36; reciprocal
obligation expectations and, 87–88;
relocation to ethnic homeland, 123;
strategic in-betweenness and, 16–17;
terminology, 21–22
second-tier Chinese cities, 143n58
Segal, Marcia Texler, 98
Shanghainese (language), 28, 29
sheng nü (leftover women), 99, 102–104
Singapore, 2, 103
Sixteen Candles (1984 film) (Hughes), 108
SK-II ad campaign video, 102–103
social issues: leveraging by ABCs,
124–125; social ambiguity, 124–125;
social capital from United States, 123;
social class and intersectionality, 126;
social distancing from local women,
118; social inequality, 126; social
landscape transformation, 134; social
networking, 128
solidarity, cross-racial, 131
Song, Miri, 62
Sophia (participant), 68, 113, 120–121
South Korea: Asian male ancestral
homeland migrants, 110; English
teachers in, 21; gender dynamics in,
106; marital statistics for women in,
103; Parasite (2020 film) (Bong), 118;
South Koreans in China, 141n2;
special visa status in, 19

Stephanie (participant), 79, 83
stereotypes: college experiences of,
42–44; as high-educated professionals, 10; negative stereotypes, 26–27,
57–58; Yellow peril representations,
8–9, 24, 129. See also model minority
myth
Steve (participant), 37, 54, 88–89,
111, 114
strategic in-betweenness in the
workplace: bypassing the bamboo
ceiling, 57–62, 107, 126; defined, 14; as
deployed by elite migrants, 124; effect
of China's global ascendance on, 134;
encouraging critical thinking, 70–73;
global economic shifts and, 7;
invoking Americanness in Chinese
workplaces, 65–70; motivations for
moving to China, 50–57; overview,
23, 49–50, 73–74; profiting from
flexible ethnicity in PRC, 62–65;
social nuance and, 124
strategic switching, 15
study abroad in young adulthood:
author's experience of, 1–2, 5;
connecting to roots, 44–47
Suh, Stephen Cho, 108
Switzerland, relocations to, 126
symbolic ethnicity, 63

Taiwan: Chinese ancestry groups in,
19–20; Chinese migrants to, 3, 80;
culturally Chinese as being from, 31;
early homeland trips with family to,
31, 39–40; as emotional homeland, 52;
gendered experiences in, 115, 120;
Kuomintang Party (KMT), 19–20;
language use, 28, 29; U.S. emigration
from, 9
Taiwanese: competition from, 94;
culturally Chinese as being from,
80–81; as ethnic option, 124;
identifying as, 13, 19–20; relocations
to, 126
Taiwanese (language), 28, 30

Taiwanese Americans: as ABCs, 141n3; in China, 78, 80; emotional belonging, 52, 55; ethnic enclaves of, 35, 38, 39–40; gendered experiences of, 112; identifying as, 20, 37; participants, 13, 35–37, *136*; Wen Ho Lee, 130

Tan, Lin, 98

Texas Sam's Club stabbing, 130

Thousand Talent Program, 18

Tony (participant), 85–86

trade war, 8, 91, 131, 132

trailing spouses, 98–99

transnationalism: belonging and, 7, 124; defined, 15; early homeland trips with family and, 30–32; field of, 16; second-generation ABCs' childhoods and, 27–28

Trieu, Monica M., 40

Trump, Donald J., 129, 131

Trump administration, 8, 26, 91, 131, 132, 133

Tsuda, Takeyuki, 73

Tuan, Mia, 63

Tu Weiming, 90, 124

U.S.-China relations: COVID-19 and, 131; progressively adversarial nature of, 24, 123, 131; trade war, 131; world-power status and, 133

U.S. Immigration and Nationality Act of 1965, 10

Vasquez, Jessica, 63

Vietnam: dating and marriage practices of, 110; dual citizenship, 18

waishengren (people from other provinces), 19, 20

Wang, L. Ling-chi, 12

Wank, David, 87

WeChat, 114, 135

Wenzhounese (language), 29

white mainstream society: America as, 8–9, 78–79, 89; Asian portrayals in, 77, 129; cultural acceptance in, 28, 129, 131; cultural assimilation to, 1, 47; downplaying ethnic heritage in, 32–35, 47; flexible ethnicity, 62–63; gendered experiences and, 108–109; marginalization in, 32–33, 36, 130; perceived differences from, 11, 25, 27, 83; white privilege, 10; white supremacy, 129. *See also* racist discourse

Wolf Warrior 2 (2017 film), 132–133

workplace issues: gender egalitarianism at work, 104–107; work styles, 73–74. *See also* strategic in-betweenness in the workplace

Wu, Elizabeth, 13–14

Wuhan, China, 129

xenophobia, 37, 78, 129

Xi Jinping, 9, 132

Yamashiro, Jane, 22

Yellow Peril representations, 8–9, 24, 129

Yeoh, Brenda, 85

Yoo, Hyung Chol, 10

Zheng, Tiantian, 113

Zheng, Victor, 75, 76

zhongguoren (native-born Chinese citizens), 17

zhongwen xuexiao (Chinese school) classes, 29–30

Zhou, Min, 29

Zhou Qunfei, 101

Zippel, Kathrin, 60

About the Author

LESLIE KIM WANG is an associate professor of sociology at the University of Massachusetts Boston. She received her PhD from the Department of Sociology at the University of California, Berkeley. Her research centers on issues of migration, gender, and family that connect the People's Republic of China with the United States. Wang is also the author of *Outsourced Children: Orphanage Care and Adoption in Globalizing China*, published in 2016.